BRITAIN IN OLD PHOTOGRAPHS

GREAT BRIDGE
& DISTRICT

TERRY PRICE

SUTTON PUBLISHING LIMITED

Sutton Publishing Limited
Phoenix Mill · Thrupp · Stroud
Gloucestershire · GL5 2BU

First published 2000

Reprinted in 2000

Title page photograph: The site of the original 'Great Bridge' over the River Tame, situated to the rear of the Kwiksave supermarket car park. The origins of this bridge have been lost in the mists of time but a crossing, possibly a wooden structure, may have existed as far back as Saxon times. (T.J.H. Price)

British Library Cataloguing in Publication Data
A catalogue record for this book is available from the British Library.

ISBN 0-7509-2495-0

Typeset in 10.5/13.5 Photina.
Typesetting and origination by
Sutton Publishing Limited.
Printed and bound in England
by J.H. Haynes & Co. Ltd, Sparkford.

*Dedicated to the memory of my mother and father,
Martha Ann and John Henry Price, who gave me so much*

All royalties received by the author from this book will be donated to the following churches in the Great Bridge area:

Great Bridge Street Methodist Church
New Road Methodist Church
Salem United Reform Church
St Pauls Church
St Peters Church

CONTENTS

Market Day in Great Bridge, 22 September 1971. This extremely popular 150-year-old market was relocated to the corner of Mill Street, Horseley Heath but was not a success. Despite appeals from the local community it never returned to its original site. (*Birmingham Post & Mail*)

An aerial view of Great Bridge Market Place, showing the Limerick Inn in the centre and what remains of the old Great Western Railway track on the right, 20 May 1975. The buildings shown in Market Street and New Road have long since disappeared to make way for a traffic island on the Great Bridge Relief Road. (*Birmingham Post & Mail*)

INTRODUCTION

Great Bridge, despite having a Tipton postal address, has the unusual distinction of being geographically situated half in Tipton and half in West Bromwich, the River Tame next to the West Bromwich Building Society being the border. Even though it has never had the status of a town, it has always been regarded as an area with a highly individual identity and at one time an industrial, manufacturing and shopping district of considerable importance. At its peak of prosperity, many of the firms and businessmen in the surrounding areas of Golds Hill, Greets Green, Horseley Heath and Toll End frequently advertised their address as 'Great Bridge, Staffordshire' rather than Tipton or West Bromwich.

How then did this small district of the Black Country rise to such prominence, competing on almost equal terms in the commercial world with many of the nearby 'official' towns? Undoubtedly the Industrial Revolution of the eighteenth and nineteenth centuries played a major part in the area's fortunes, but let us look back even further to see how Great Bridge came into being.

Between 1180 and 1700 various legal documents have recorded no fewer than six different spellings of 'Great' and since then many theories have been put forward concerning the origin of the name. It is impossible to say with any degree of certainty when a bridge first appeared across the River Tame at this point or how the area came to be known as 'Great', but the most popular and widely accepted explanation is that as the locality was once made up of large deposits of gravel and the word 'grete' or 'greet' was used to describe this, its association with the bridge eventually produced the name 'Greet Bridge'.

The main road through Great Bridge has not always followed the course of the present highway. It used to continue in a straight line past Whitehall Road, over wasteland, crossing what was later to become Slater Street and Fisher Street, towards the small bridge which is now situated to the rear of the Kwiksave supermarket. This is the original 'Great' Bridge which has been on the site for hundreds of years; of course, it has been rebuilt a number of times.

By 1550 the first recorded settlement had occurred on the West Bromwich side of the bridge, although there was already a mill owned by Sandwell Priory dating from the twelfth century on the Tipton part. In 1646 Oliver Cromwell's Parliamentary Forces led by Sir William Brereton crossed over this 'Great' Bridge on their way to lay siege to Dudley Castle, which later surrendered without any fighting taking place.

Because of the importance of this crossing, Staffordshire County in 1699 assigned £50 towards the cost of its conversion from a horse bridge to a stone cart bridge. West Bromwich, however, refused to join Tipton in carrying out the work and in 1702 the Courts ordered those concerned to repay £20 and spend the remaining £30 on the

Tipton half and the causeway leading to it. It is interesting to note that around this time the road through Great Bridge was being described as 'the great road between London, Chester and Shrewsbury'. The change in the name from 'Greet' to 'Great', which also dates from this period, may be the result of this reference.

During the eighteenth century the development of coal-consuming industries saw coal-mining growing rapidly in the area, and with it the need for an improvement in local transport. As a result of this increased traffic, in 1752 a new, much wider bridge was built further along the Tame, which necessitated the realignment of the main highway near to Whitehall Road and at Horseley Heath to form the route we know today. The 'New Road' was probably constructed at the same time. The coach from London to Shrewsbury was now able to pass through Great Bridge and by 1771 a tollgate had been erected near to the junction with Whitehall Road. A tollhouse was also built close by on the corner of Slater Street. As a reminder of those early coaching days a milestone could be seen in Great Bridge Street outside the offices of Muntz & Barwell as recently as the 1960s.

The landscape of Great Bridge in the early nineteenth century was changing dramatically as the coalmines, ironworks and manufacturing industries which covered the area began to produce at an ever increasing rate. For example, in 1836 Messrs Haines and Horton drew from one pair of pits at Cop Hall Colliery, in one week, 1,000 tons of coal, then an English record. As the population grew, so did the number of chapels and schools surrounding what was becoming a centre of commerce. Shops and Inns were starting to appear and a market was established in front of the Limerick.

The second half of the century saw the building of two railway stations in Great Bridge, on the South Staffordshire Line in 1850 and on the GWR in 1866, which together with the introduction of a tram service between Birmingham and Great Bridge in 1872 further enhanced the potential for increased trade and prosperity in the area.

Between 1900 and 1950 Great Bridge reached the peak of its size and popularity, with an abundance of manufacturing firms and privately owned shops where you could buy practically anything from bicycles to ice cream, all made on the premises. Many of the local industries became world famous, such as Braithwaites, Conex Sanbra, Horseley Bridge & Thomas Piggott, Muntz & Barwell, Ratcliffs, Triplex, and the Wellington Tube Works. Farley Park provided a venue for leisure activities such as crown green bowling, cricket, football and tennis, while in the summer months concerts were held in the bandstand. The centre of entertainment, however, was the Palace Cinema, affectionately known as 'The Bug Ole', where you were invited by a large poster outside to 'bring your Alice to our Palace'. What memories this picture house conjures up for everyone who went there.

In the 1960s the Palace Cinema, along with a number of adjacent buildings, was demolished and replaced by a row of modern shops. Since then Great Bridge has continued to be redeveloped, and new retail outlets now occupy the sites of once famous household names.

I am sure that the photographs in this book will bring back happy memories to all those who, like me, knew Great Bridge in its heyday and will, I hope, also in some small way enable present and future generations to see what the area and its people were like in times gone by.

Terence J.H. Price
3 April 2000

CHAPTER ONE

SHOPS, MARKETS & STREETS

Arthur and Minnie Welch stand outside their ladies' and gents' outfitters at 2 & 3 New Road, Great Bridge, *c.* 1925. The trio on the right of the picture are, from left to right: Doris Welch, -?-, Doris Williams. The business, which was established in 1908, was later extended to include the next door property at No. 4. When the Tipton Municipal Borough was created in 1938 Arthur Welch had the honour of becoming its first Mayor. He died in 1969 aged eighty-two, just two years after the closure of his New Road shop. (Beryl Jarvis)

A lady hurries away from a crowded market in the centre of Great Bridge, *c.* 1910. An open market had been on the site in front of the Limerick Inn since the early part of the nineteenth century. After the move to nearby Mill Street in the early 1970s shopping in Great Bridge was never quite the same again. (Ken Rock)

Comedian Larry Grayson opens the new seventy stall Great Bridge covered and open air market, in October 1979. His arrival in a Rolls-Royce brought traffic to a standstill and attracted hundreds of shoppers to the event. The organiser, Ted Skett, had invested £15,000 to convert a warehouse at the back of 55 to 63 Great Bridge into a market hall in an effort to bring back shoppers to the area. (*Birmingham Post & Mail*)

A busy Great Bridge market scene, with John Gilson's Boot Shop prominent in the background, *c.* 1915. His recently painted wall sign is proclaiming the fact that he has been in business for fifty years and that working mens' boots are a speciality. The tall building on the left of the picture was the second shop to be opened in Great Bridge by grocer George Mason. (Ken Rock)

Robert Kennedy draws the crowds to his stall on the new Great Bridge market as he offers a cauliflower to shopper Barbara Aston, October 1979. The market, which replaced the unpopular Mill Street site, has proved to be very successful and has been enlarged several times since. (*Birmingham Post & Mail*)

John Bell, baker and grocer, stands in the doorway of his shop at 220 Great Bridge Street, *c.* 1910. The business was established in 1854 and traded for over 100 years before the premises became a DIY store around 1958. John, who was a popular figure in the area, was also a local councillor, and in 1921 he became the Mayor of West Bromwich. (Ned Williams)

Miss Beattie Warren pictured in December 1956 inside the newsagent and hairdressing shop at 70 Great Bridge, which she jointly ran with her brother Clifford from 1913 to 1958. Her father Walter established the business at 116 New Road in the 1870s, and by 1904 he had moved to larger premises at No. 1, near the Market Place. (Philip Evans)

The premises of William Powell, cycle and motor dealer 123–4 Horseley Heath, Great Bridge, *c.* 1930. Although the picture has seen better days it is nevertheless an interesting view of this well-known business, which was originally established in the late nineteenth century a few doors away at No. 139. The firm, which was later run by Albert and Harry Powell, survived until the early 1970s when the building was demolished and replaced by an open market. (Alan Price)

Miss Brenda Dodd stands in the doorway of Bannister & Thatcher, chemist in Great Bridge, *c.* 1955. The firm was established in the 1920s by a Mr Bannister and a Mr Thatcher who had previously been running their own separate pharmacy businesses in the Walsall area. By the time they had sold out to Lloyds chemist in the early 1980s the number of branches in the Birmingham and Black Country areas had grown to around twenty-six. (Brenda Nicklin)

Sylvia Gould's grocery shop, 40 Horseley Road, Great Bridge, *c.* 1920. During the early part of the twentieth century various members of the Gould family appear to have had a wide range of business interests in the Tipton and West Bromwich areas. Sylvia's father Solomon, for example, was an insurance agent in Toll End in 1904 before moving four years later to Eagle Road, where he became landlord of the Swan Tavern. At the same time he was also trading as a coal dealer from Great Bridge Wharf. By 1916, however, the family were residing at the Horseley Road premises, where his wife Mary, pictured in the doorway, was recorded as being the registered owner, passing on the business shortly afterwards to her daughter Sylvia. Another member of the Gould family, also named Sylvia, was listed between 1904 and 1921 in West Bromwich variously as a beer retailer at 91 High Street, a shopkeeper in Hall End and again a beer retailer at 34 Paradise Street and 109 Phoenix Street. The shop in Horseley Road, which was situated next door to the Rising Sun public house, was eventually sold in about 1930 to a lady by the name of Martha Jane Starkey. (Sylvia Belhartley)

George Martin and his family (right) stand outside their fish, poultry and foreign fruit shop at 118 New Road, Great Bridge during the coronation celebrations of King George V, June 1911. Next door at No. 117 on the left of the picture are the boot and shoe premises of Benjamin Sowry. The young lad in the right foreground with a cap is George Matthews. His cousin Ernie Smith is next to him. (Mary Law)

Fruiterer and grocer Walter Kendall pictured inside his shop at 118 New Road, Great Bridge in 1950, having just completed a major reconstruction and enlargement of the premises, which also absorbed the property next door at No. 119. The business, which was acquired in 1940 from the previous owner Mrs Lily Jones, had the distinction of being the first in Great Bridge to sell frozen food. In August 1970 Walter also purchased G. Bonaccorsi's confectionery shop at 120 New Road. Within three and a half years, however, both shops had been forced to close because of proposed roadworks by the local council, Kendall's fruiterers in 1972 and Bonaccorsi's confectionery on 31 December 1973. (Walter Kendall)

William Reynolds pictured outside his hairdressing and newsagents shop at 127 Horseley Heath, with his sister May on the left, *c.* 1907. William, who was an astute businessman, had opened these premises in 1903 when he was only seventeen years old! Such was his success that by 1912 the business had moved to more spacious accommodation at 33 Market Place, Great Bridge where William, now married, in addition to his newsagent and hairdressing interests established a dolls' hospital and an umbrella repair service. In 1950 his son Walter, and daughter-in-law Hazel joined the business, and during the following years they modernised and greatly enlarged the trading area. Following William's death in 1967 at the age of eighty-one the business, under the ownership of Walter and Hazel, continued to flourish, and in 1976 it was further expanded when the next door property of Harold Moult's sports shop was acquired. Shortly afterwards they began selling bicycles after Raleigh had appointed them their main agents in the area, following the closure of Powell's cycle shop in Horseley Heath. In 1983, however, the business was sold, thus bringing to an end a hundred years of trading in Great Bridge by the Reynolds family. (Walter Reynolds)

Beedle & Son, ironmongers at 10 Market Place, Great Bridge, *c.* 1910. The origin of the firm dates from around 1870 when John Beedle started trading from this address as a hosier and haberdasher. However, by the turn of the century trade directories were showing the proprietor as Mrs Elizabeth Beedle who dealt in fancy goods and hardware. During the late 1920s the business transferred next door to No. 11 which had been occupied by Edward Hipkins, pork butcher, part of whose shop can be seen on the right of the picture. Known in the locality as 'Cheap Jacks', Beedle & Son continued to operate until 1951 when it was taken over by the Wolverhampton firm of Hughes and Holmes Ltd. (Hughes & Holmes Ltd)

When this picture was taken in about 1951 the premises of hardware dealers Beedle & Son, at 11 Market Place, Great Bridge, had just been taken over by the firm of Hughes & Holmes Ltd. Their business was established on 1 April 1923 at Wolverhampton by Messrs George Hughes and Henry Holmes, the latter partner leaving in the early 1940s after being bought out. The Great Bridge premises have been considerably enlarged over the years and the frontage extended by absorbing the properties at Nos 9 and 10 which, after internal alteration, has greatly increased the trading area. (Hughes & Holmes Ltd)

A.H. Hodson, corn and seed merchant, New Road, Great Bridge, *c.* 1958. When Albert Hodson started trading at 6 New Road in 1937 he occupied only the right half of the property pictured above, the previous owner being Withnalls the hatters. During the early 1950s he also purchased the building at No. 5 (left), thus enabling him to expand the frontage to that seen above. The business closed in 1969 when he was forced to retire, owing to ill health. (Philip Evans)

Outside the premises of Bagnalls Outfitters at 119–20 Horseley Heath, *c.* 1913. Left to right: William Bagnall, Edwin Bagnall, Lucy Bagnall, Elizabeth Reynolds. This well-known business was originally established by Francis Reynolds in property known as Jubilee Buildings at 135 Horseley Heath in 1888. Elizabeth Reynolds was the mother of Lucy Bagnall, whose brother William Reynolds was a well-known Great Bridge newsagent. During the 1930s and 1940s Lucy Bagnall represented the Horseley Heath Ward on the Tipton Council and from 1941 to 1943 was the Deputy Mayor. The business, which was jointly owned by Lucy and her husband William, closed in the 1970s after more than ninety years' trading in the Great Bridge area. (Eileen Whitehouse)

Giuseppe Bonaccorsi with two of the five horse-drawn ice cream carts operated by his son Peter from their confectionery business in New Road, Great Bridge, *c.* 1928. Giuseppe, who adopted the name Joseph, began trading in partnership with his son Peter from a small shop at 7 New Road in 1913. Before long it became necessary to find larger premises where the manufacture of their popular ice cream could be increased, and so around 1920 they moved the short distance to No. 120 on the opposite side of New Road. In the years that followed Joseph's death in 1930 the horse-drawn and tricycle carts were gradually replaced with a fleet of motor vans. Ice cream production continued to increase until in 1948 a new factory was built, which was run by Peter's brothers Maurizio (George) and Marcello (Mark). From 1954 until his death in 1971 George Bonaccorsi also ran the Market Place Café, his son Michael carrying on the business until it was sold in 1995. Peter Bonaccorsi died in 1962 but his ice cream and confectionery business continued until, in 1970, it was purchased by fruiterer Walter Kendall, whose wife Marie ran the shop until it eventually closed in 1973. (Cynthia Bonaccorsi)

Staff at the grocery business of Mason, Williams & Co. Ltd, 68 Great Bridge, pose for a photograph, *c.* 1905. The firm was part owned by George Mason who had bought himself into the business during the early years of the twentieth century. After setting up his own company in 1909 and opening his first shop in Birmingham, it was not long before he had branches throughout the country. By the time of his death in 1934 the number of 'George Mason' shops had expanded to five hundred. (Philip Evans)

Chrissy Taylor's fruiterer's shop at 126 Horseley Heath, 1938. Built in 1936 to replace their previous shop on this site, which had been demolished a year earlier, the business had originally been opened in 1928 as a general store. Pictured standing outside the shop is Chrissy's brother Walter Kendall, who from 1940 until 1972 ran his own fruiterer's at 118 New Road. (Walter Kendall)

Ball's shop at 88 Cophall Street, close to Richardsons coal yard, *c.* 1920. It was typical of many general stores in the area where the front rooms of terraced houses were converted into small shops. This one was not very successful, however, as William and Eliza Ball were 'too kind' to some of their customers, allowing the non-payment of goods obtained on the 'strap' to get out of hand. The business finally closed in 1934. In the picture from left to right are daughters Gladys Ball and Alice Ball, with mother Eliza Ball completing the trio. (Elsie Pritchard)

Albert Downes stands outside his café and general stores at 1 Charles Street, 1946. Situated on the corner adjoining Phoenix Street, the front room operated as the stores while in the café at the back breakfast or lunch, including a cup of tea, would have set you back 9*d*. Albert, assisted by his wife Winnie, ran this very successful business for ten years before moving on in 1956 to take over another café in the Hill Top area of West Bromwich. (Ian Downes)

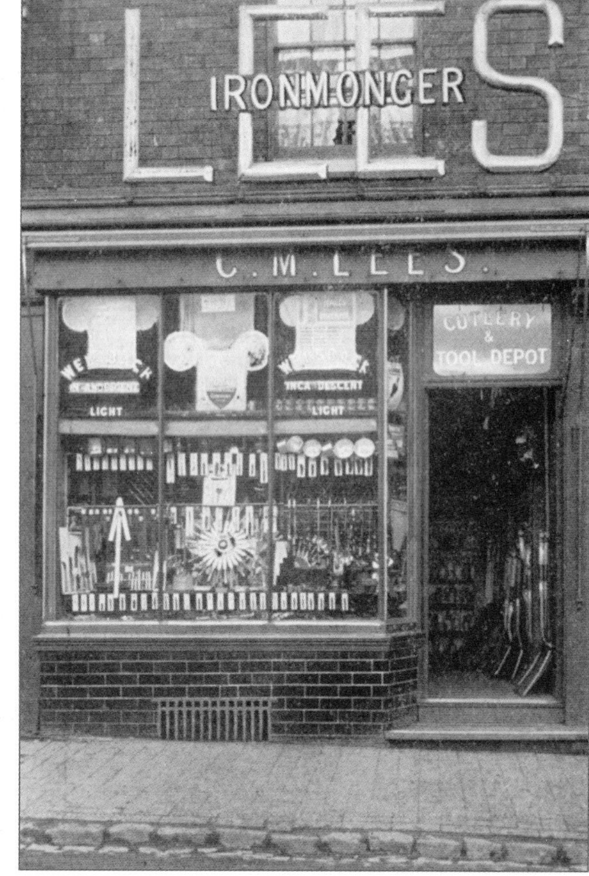

The frontage of Charles M. Lees at 109 and 110 New Road, Great Bridge, *c.* 1910. Advertising himself as a general and manufacturing ironmonger, the size of his shop did not do justice to the many and varied services offered. Presumably one of the two properties he occupied was a workshop because he also carried out motor-cycle, car, traction engine and lorry repairs there. He was also one of the few people in the Great Bridge area advertising driving lessons to the general public. (T.J.H. Price)

Elizabeth Reynolds stands in the doorway of her clothier's shop in Jubilee Buildings, Horseley Heath, *c.* 1902. The business, which was established in 1888, was later passed on to her daughter and son-in-law Lucy and William Bagnall. Just in view on the right of the picture is Joe Adams' fruit and greengrocery shop, while on the left are the premises of beer retailer J.H. Hughes. (Eileen Whitehouse)

A view of the Market Place, Great Bridge, *c.* 1905, looking towards Horseley Heath with the Wesleyan chapel on the left and the Limerick Inn on the right. John Parry the Cash Tailor can be seen displaying his cloth, while the large flagpole is outside the boot and shoe premises of John Gilson. (Ken Rock)

Great Bridge Market Place, *c.* 1903. The tall corner building in the centre of the picture is Daniel Hipkins' Meat Stores with, at the side, a passage leading down to Railway View. Next door can be seen a pair of steps hanging from the frontage of Beedles' the Ironmongers, while other shops in the picture include Hymen Cohen, tailor; Philip Gavin, draper; Augustine Nelthorpe, watchmaker; and Thomas Turner's Coffee House. (Ken Rock)

A view across the Market Place, Great Bridge, *c.* 1925. Just beyond the Limerick Inn on the left with its magnificent lantern can be seen the picture framing and fancy goods store of Saxons & Co. at No. 1 New Road. Further along from the Union Supply on the right are the shaded premises of W. Devis & Sons Ltd, Butchers, and Florence Wynn, Ladies' Outfitters. (Philip Evans)

The Market Place, Great Bridge, *c.* 1903. Within the following twenty years the boot shop of Thomas Collins, pictured here on the left, had been demolished and replaced by a much taller building, later occupied by W. Devis & Sons Ltd, butchers. The large 'Sale' sign is one of a pair either side of the premises of Ryder & Sons, draper and hosier. In the distance is the post office building, while the magnificent edifice seen on the right belongs to the Stork Inn. (Jim Houghton)

W. Devis & Sons Ltd, butchers, occupy the site of Thomas Collins' Boot Shop in this view of Great Bridge Market Place photographed in the late 1940s, while next door Ryder & Sons have also been replaced by the ladies' outfitting business of Florence Wynn. Among the shops on the opposite side are grocers George Mason and wine and spirit merchant Frank Tittley. (Jim Houghton)

The New Road in Great Bridge pictured above was closed for several days in May 1977 when the premises of G. Bonaccorsi became unsafe and had to be demolished along with Walter Kendall's fruiterers and grocery shop. The buildings had remained empty since they had ceased trading in 1973. (*Birmingham Post & Mail*)

New Road, Great Bridge viewed from the Market Place in 1955, showing Giuseppe Bonaccorsi's ice cream and confectionery business and the Union Supply Co. on the right. The railway bridge in the background carried the Great Western branch line from Swan Village to Great Bridge, which opened in 1866. By 1964, almost a hundred years later, its passenger service had ceased. Today a traffic island is situated where the bridge and the shops in the picture once stood. (Philip Evans)

The junction of the New Road and the Market Place, Great Bridge, *c.* 1903. This picture postcard was produced by the printing firm of Thomas Blackham, seen here on the extreme right, who were one of the few early Great Bridge businesses to survive into the 1960s. The grocery shop of the Union Supply Co. was locally owned, as was Farmer's Hatters and Hosiers. (Janice Endean)

Another view of New Road, Great Bridge, *c.* 1910, showing how extremely dirty the roads and the pavements were in those 'good old days'. Note the block and steps leading to the elevated front door of No. 119 on the right of the picture, while just behind can be seen a number of rabbits hanging outside the fish and poultry business of George Martin at 118 New Road. (Ian Bott)

Jacob Reynolds stands in the doorway of his Hairdressing & Shaving Saloon, Great Bridge, with on the left of the picture Limerick Passage (afterwards Market Street), *c.* 1905. The large upper-storey Odd Fellows hall situated behind the Reynolds' building was later used as a cinema, a licence being issued by Tipton UDC in 1910. This pre-dated the Palace and the Victoria cinemas by two years. (Walter Reynolds)

An unusual view of the Market Place, Great Bridge, *c.* 1925. The large lantern on the left of the picture is hanging from the side of the Limerick Inn while across the road, on the corner of the entrance to Thomas Cox's sawmill, are the shaded premises of the Home and Colonial Tea Stores. (Philip Evans)

The post office, Great Bridge, on the corner of Brickhouse Lane, *c.* 1905. Known locally as Caxton House, it was the home of Charles and Marianne Purser from 1890 until 1933. They had eight children, one of whom, Marie was still alive in 1990 aged 102! (Jim Houghton)

A virtually empty Great Bridge looking towards Charlie's Café in the distance on the corner of Whitehall Road, *c.* 1975. Opposite Brickhouse Lane, on the right of the picture, are the premises of George Hipkins, Family Butchers, with a 'For Sale' board outside. (Frank Wardle)

The West Bromwich half of the main road running through Great Bridge as it was in 1903, looking towards the Wagon & Horses Hotel on the left and Whitehall Road in the distance. The protruding building in the centre of the picture is the old eighteenth-century tollhouse which was demolished around 1910. (Ken Rock)

This view of the main road on the West Bromwich side of Great Bridge dates from about 1925, when the Warren family commissioned a series of high quality postcard scenes of the area. Brothers Clifford and Charles Warren can just be seen under the barber's pole looking out from the doorway of their newsagents shop, next door to the Stork Inn on the right of the picture. To the left of Warren's is grocer George Mason's shop with the Lion Inn and George Hipkins Family Butcher Ltd further along. (Philip Evans)

Great Bridge from the junction with Fisher Street, looking towards the West Bromwich border with Tipton at the River Tame bridge, *c.* 1905. On the left of the picture is the Clothing Company of Foster Brothers and to the right just beyond Brickhouse Lane are the premises of Thomas Davis, corn merchant. (Ken Rock)

Great Bridge at the junction with Slater Street, *c.* 1925. Just in view to the left of the picture is the entrance to the Palace Cinema with, above, a statuette of Eros. Horton's Bakery can also be seen on the opposite corner. The imposing building on the right, with five windows in each of the upper storeys, was once mainly occupied by saddle and harness makers C. & S. Baggott. In this photograph, however, it is three separate shops. Next door, but set back from the road, is the Wagon & Horses Hotel and, on the extreme right, the Whitehall Cycle Co. (Philip Evans)

The main Great Bridge road at its junction with Whitehall Road, February 1964. The shops on the left alongside Victor Value occupy the site of the old Palace Cinema, which closed in 1960. Further along on the corner of Slater Street can be seen the Great Bridge branch of F.W. Woolworth & Co. Ltd, which opened during the 1950s. (David Wilson)

The junction of Whitehall Road and the main Great Bridge thoroughfare, May 1971. The shop displaying the 'For Sale' board was once New Era Decorators' Supplies, which was established in 1947 by Frank Cormell. Next door at No. 13 was the Queens fish and chip shop with Purnell's, the newsagent, at No. 9. On the extreme right of the picture at No. 1 was Miss Nellie Hall's sweetshop. (Alf Perks)

None of the buildings in this picture of Whitehall Road in July 1968 has survived to the present day. The houses on the left date from the nineteenth century while those on the right, between Sheepwash Lane and Farley Street, were built in the early twentieth century on land adjoining the old Cop Hall. (Alan Price)

Whitehall Road, Greets Green, at its junction with Whitgreave Street, 13 April 1964. A 'For Sale' notice is displayed outside the premises of the Dunkirk Brewery. To the right of the picture, near the 'Bundy Clock', is a West Bromwich Corporation Daimler bus operating on the short Great Bridge to Dartmouth Square route. (David Wilson)

Fisher Street, Great Bridge, looking from the Sheepwash Lane end towards the Royal Exchange pub in the distance, *c.* 1904. The grocery shop on the left of the picture, behind the gas lamp, was run by William and Rachel Burton while Abraham Stubbs the coal merchant is further down at No. 93. The street dates from 1859 and takes its name from the Fisher family who had lived in the area for centuries. (T.J.H. Price)

Elwell Street, Great Bridge, July 1976. The row of buildings seen here once contained two general stores, one run by Ethel and Maud Parsons at No. 53 (fifth house from the corner) and the other by Evelyn Sansome at No. 35 (just beyond the two parked cars). At the bottom of the street was the entrance to the Wellington Tube Works sports ground. The street was laid out in about 1855 on land previously known as Elwell Fields. (T.J.H. Price)

CHAPTER TWO

PUBS & CUSTOMERS

The outward appearance of the Rising Sun in Horseley Road, Great Bridge, has changed very little since this picture was taken in 1935. 'Mine Host' at the time was Walter Randall, only the seventh licensee to occupy the premises since George Webb became the first in about 1860. In 1999 the present licensees, Penny McDonald and Jackie Walker, saw their pub named in the CAMRA *Good Beer Guide* as the best in the country after winning a national competition. (Penny McDonald/Jackie Walker)

The Stork Inn, Great Bridge, *c.* 1979. The inn dates from the early nineteenth century when Frederick Farley was the landlord. Standing on the West Bromwich side of the River Tame in Great Bridge, and famous for its superb bowling green at the rear, the inn eventually closed around 1985. The Kwiksave supermarket now occupies the site. (Robin Pearson)

The Leopard Inn, on the corner of Meeting Street and Horseley Heath, July 1968. Originally a nineteenth century 'home brew' beer house, made up from two separate houses, the pub was eventually acquired and upgraded by Mitchells & Butlers Ltd. It was subsequently demolished around 1976. (Alan Price)

The Lion at 66 Great Bridge, *c.* 1930. It was better known as 'Lucas's' after long-standing landlord Charles Lucas and his wife Ada who occupied the premises from around 1910 until 1947. The first licence, however, appears to have been held in the late 1800s by a Mrs Charlotte Silvester, who was described at the time as a retailer of ale, porter and cider. After licensee John Greenhalgh and his wife Mary had closed the doors for the last time in 1956 the property was acquired for development by their neighbour, George Hipkins Ltd, family butcher. Other well-known landlords have been Howard Hughes and Teddy England. (Robin Pearson/Jean Wade)

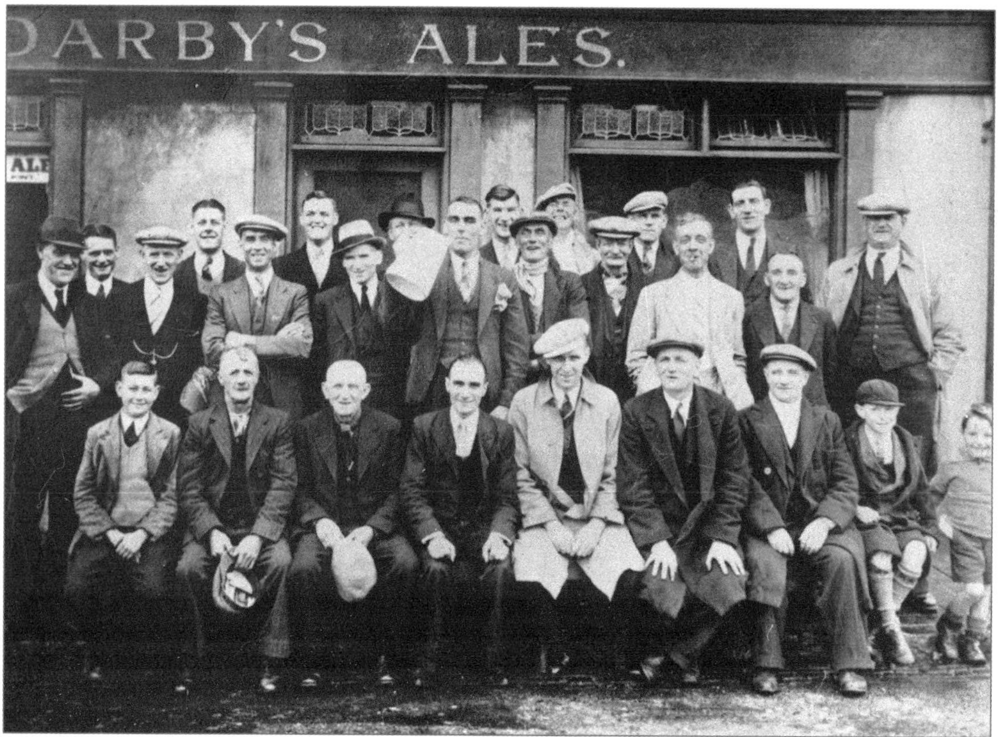

A gathering of locals outside the Britannia Inn, Pikehelve Street, Golds Hill, *c.* 1940. This was a Darby's house often referred to as 'Merthers'. Back row, left to right: -?-, -?-, Len Beesley, Douglas Hill, William Price, Bert Faulkner, Fred James, William Merther (licensee), Arthur Willoughby, Tom James, Charles Willoughby, Harry Cowles, Joe Aldridge, -?-, Arthur Price, Sam Jones, William Mullaney, Charles Mogg. Front row: Robert James, Jack Edmunds, Thomas Lloyd, -?-, Edward Burgess, Jack Hughes, Thomas Harper, Maurice Beesley, Kenneth Mullaney. (Albert Murphy)

The Wagon & Horses Commercial Hotel, Great Bridge, *c.* 1935. Built in 1764 to cater for the increase in coach traffic, these were the oldest licensed premises in the area. The landlord at the time of this photograph was William H. Morrissey who was advertising trips to Windsor and Ascot Races at 12*s* 6*d* on a board outside the bar. On the left of the picture, Peggy's Ladies' Hairdressing, run by Phyllis Perkins, was offering permanent waving for 8*s* 6*d*. (David Whyley)

The lounge of the Royal Oak, Whitehall Road, Great Bridge, late 1950s. In the background a poster advertises the appearance of Cliff Richard at the Dudley Hippodrome. At the back on the left are Tony and Iris Welch. Centre: Tommy Meek and Tony Green; bottom left: Tommy Hubble with, behind him, Sid Morris; second from right: Stan Downing; fourth from right: Freddy Jones; fifth from right: Ray White. (Lyn Elwell)

The Whitehall Tavern, Whitehall Road, Greets Green, with the entrance to Farley Park shown on the right, July 1968. Prior to its demolition in September 1969, the building had remained empty since it was last occupied by licensee Edward Carter in 1958. The property was first owned by Samuel Dudley who in 1880 was also the landlord of the Royal Exchange in nearby Cape Street. The 'Tavern' was at one time also known as Whitehall House, which tends to suggest that it was originally a private residence. (Alan Price)

Customers of the Royal Oak, Whitehall Road, Great Bridge, *c.* 1957, with their cup winning domino team, which played in the Greets Green League. Behind the bar are licensees Ted and Ann Penny. In front of the dartboard are Horace Davis and Nellie Howes; and on the extreme right is Sam Price. Front row, left to right: -?-, Wilf Evans, Arthur Howes, Fred Rollinson, Alf Gilson. (Lyn Elwell)

The Rose & Crown, Cape Street, Greets Green, when John Hadley was the licensee, July 1968. Originally two separate buildings, the pub dates from the mid-nineteenth century when landlord Sam Lavender kept it. Other well-known occupants during the early 1900s were William Dunn and William Gamble. (Alan Price)

Pictured behind the bar of the Rose & Crown public house in Cape Street, Greets Green, *c.* 1930, are Hannah Gamble, John Edwards and licensee William Gamble. The large trophy on the right was won by their bowling team who, along with the jazz band and shooting club, amassed a total of eleven cups during the period 1921–31. (Jean Beddow)

The Royal Exchange at 33 Cape Street, Greets Green, *c.* 1912. Originally owned by Samuel Dudley, who in 1875 was the first landlord, the pub apparently remained in the same family until its closure around 1920. The last of the Dudley family to hold the licence was Emma, pictured here in front of the pub with her children. Back row, left to right: Emma Dudley, Samuel Dudley. Front row: Sarah Jayne Dudley, Lily Dudley, Annie Dudley. (Joyce Stimpson)

Customers at the rear of the Bulls Head pub at 29 Grout Street, Greets Green, *c.* 1930. The smart lad on the right is Howard Dunn, son of the licensee at the time, Ben Dunn. Back row, left to right: ? Wilde, -?-, Sam Pardon, Bill Hodgkisson, Tom Whale, ? Parker, -?-, Howard Dunn. Front row: Jim Slater, Sam Dudfield, David Bowen, -?-, -?-, Kneeling: -?-. (Ken Hodgkisson)

A close-up view of the Dunkirk Inn, Greets Green, *c.* 1912. Left to right: Elizabeth F. Yates and Florence M. Yates, both daughters of the licensee, George J. Yates. In 1900 Charles Darby, who was landlord of the Bush, Claypit Lane, bought Dunkirk Hall in Whitehall Road, converting part of it to the inn pictured above. Two years later he started the construction of a brewery next to the Hall in order to supply his rapidly growing chain of pubs, which proudly displayed the name Darby's Ales. (Sid Griffiths)

The bar of the Britannia Inn, Whitehall Road, Great Bridge, *c.* 1920. This is a wonderful example of the central heating system employed in many of these pubs during the early twentieth century, although this one does not seem to be working, judging by the overcoated customer on the left. The man seated at the front with a trilby hat in his lap is Sam Price; the licensee at the time was William Jones. (Cliff Price)

The Wellington Inn, Great Bridge Street, 1980s. Built around 1875, the first licensee was Thomas Chambers who by 1890 had passed it on to his daughter, Miss Mary Ann Chambers. Well known as a pigeon flyers' pub, it was curiously one of three buildings in Great Bridge Street bearing the name 'Wellington'. (T.J.H. Price)

The domino team of the Beehive, Great Bridge Street in the pub's smoke room after winning the Greets Green League, *c.* 1952. In later years the brewery named this room 'The Monkey Pen' in memory of its long serving licensee George 'Monkey' Jackson. Back row, left to right: Billy Stamps, Jim Arter, Wilf Davenport, Arthur Williams, Arthur Aston, Geoff Brookes, Gerald Cox, Jimmy Hunter. Front row: -?-, Joe Price, Arthur Dunn, Frank Turner, Alf Gilson, George Melia, Tom Yates. (Geoff Brookes)

The Britannia Inn at 317 Whitehall Road, Great Bridge, July 1968. Built in the 1830s when the old 'New Town' was being laid out (but never completed), the pub was probably best known for licensee Fred Leeson who became Mayor of West Bromwich in 1957/8. He was still in residence when this picture was taken. (Alan Price)

Customers of the Britannia Inn, Whitehall Road, Great Bridge, at the back of the premises with landlord William Jones, *c.* 1933. Back row, left to right: -?-, -?-, -?-, Albert Walker, -?-, Jim Copper, -?-. Middle row: -?-, Vincent Connor, Bill Wagstaff, -?-, -?-, -?-. Front row: William Jones, -?-, Sam Toon, ? Stott, -?-. (Lily Phillips)

Thomas Stillard is known to have been the landlord of the Prince Regent in Horseley Heath back in 1830, but it may have been an earlier building than the one pictured here in June 1969. During the first half of the twentieth century the pub was well known for having on display a large ape, which William Perry, the Tipton Slasher, is reputed to have sparred with. The premises closed in February 1991. (Alan Price)

Pictured in the doorway of the Nags Head in Great Bridge around 1930 is William T. Griffiths, landlord from 1921 until his retirement in 1936. Situated on the corner of Mill Street (right), its actual adress was 34 Market Place. During the 1990s it became fashionable to change many traditional pub names, and as a consequence this one became The Fusilier. (Maggie Ralph)

A 'ladies only' outing to Claverley from the Cop Hall Hotel, Sheepwash Lane, Great Bridge, *c.* 1910. According to a trade directory of 1835 one of the first landlords was Joseph Haines, whose business interests also included the Cop Hall Colliery. When this picture was taken, however, Joseph Taylor was the licensee, only the sixth occupant during the previous seventy-five years. (T.J.H. Price)

Regulars from the Queen's Head in Horton Street, Great Bridge, take time off to pose for a picture, *c.* 1928. They include on the back row, extreme right, Levi Bevan, and on the front row, fourth from right, Sam Price. Between 1860 and its closure in 1956 the pub had just seven licensees: Samuel Wright, Thomas Wright, Bert Clarke, William Hingley, Benjamin Morgan, Norman Dearn and John Hopkins. (Muriel Ashcroft)

The Queen's Head pub, 63 Horton Street, Great Bridge, *c.* 1956. Better known as 'Tommy Wright's' after a long-standing publican of the same name. It was originally a 'home-brew' beer house until it became part of the Darby's chain of pubs early in the last century and, according to the sign above the door, was licensed to sell only ale and cider, not spirits. The couple pictured in the doorway are landlord John Hopkins and his wife Iris, who in 1956 were the last to call time at this popular pub. The building was demolished in the late 1950s along with other property in the street. Blocks of multi-storey flats now occupy the Horton Street site. (Doris Abbotts)

A group of locals at the side of the Queen's Head pub ('Tommy Wright's'), Horton Street, Great Bridge, *c.* 1948. Back row, left to right: Sam Boxley, -?-, Simon Haywood, Jim Nock, 'Dot' Boughton, -?-, Joe Webb, -?-, Bill Ruston, -?-, Jack Evans, Bert Clarke (licensee), Les Greenfield, ? Fullwood, -?-, George Jukes, ? Fullwood, Enoch Toon, Arthur Read. Front row: Arthur May, Tom Dugmore, ? Smith, Bill Abrahams, Bill Turner, George Dixon. (Irene Stott)

The Turf Tavern, 13 Aston Street, at its junction with Hackett Street, Toll End, *c.* 1938. Landlord John Summerton and his wife Edith ran this pub from 1937 until 1939, when they moved to the new Shrubbery public house which had just been built in Horseley Road. Dating from around 1850 the Turf Tavern's first licensee was one William Fletcher. (Christine Brookes)

The Durham Ox pub in Railway Street, Horseley Heath, August 1968. At this time Charles Walker was the licensee. The pub closed around 1974 but the building still stands, unoccupied, in a street devoid of any houses. (Alan Price)

The Swan Tavern at No. 1 Eagle Road (later known as Eagle Lane), Great Bridge, *c.* 1908. An abundance of swans frequenting the many pools in the area was probably the inspiration for the pub's name and indeed, according to an 1837 John Wood map of West Bromwich, Eagle Road was originally known as Swan Street. Licensee Solomon Gould, pictured here with his family, was at the same time also carrying on the business of a coal dealer operating out of Great Bridge Wharf, having previously been an insurance agent residing at 171 Toll End Road. It seems that they were not at the Swan very long because by 1916 the landlord was listed as being one Frank Howes, and also by this time Solomon's wife Mary was running a grocery business in Horseley Road. Left to right: Sylvia Gould (daughter), Richard Gould (son). In the doorway: Mary Gould, Solomon Gould. (Sylvia Belhartley)

Regulars at the Shakespeare Inn, Bridge Road, Toll End interrupt their drinking to pose for a photograph, 18 November 1927. The licensee at the time was John Spittle, the third member of the family to run the pub since Benjamin Spittle took it over around 1910. Among those pictured are, middle row second from left, Sam Price; third from right, Bill Price; and front row extreme right, Jim Powell. (T.J.H. Price)

The Royal Exchange, 15 Fisher Street, Great Bridge, *c.* 1948. It was one of the many public houses at the time owned by Darby's Brewery Ltd of Greets Green. The premises appear to have been first licensed during the late nineteenth century when a George Watson became landlord. Some years later he presumably passed the property on to another member of his family because by 1921 the licence was being held by one Sarah Jane Watson. Only one further licensee (Herbert Cole) is known before Frederick Aston and his wife Violet took it over in the late 1930s. The pub remained in their hands for over twenty-five years before finally closing around 1966. (Robin Pearson)

The Rose & Crown, Pikehelve Street, Golds Hill, dates from the 1890s, when one Henry Portsmouth was noted as the first landlord. Many of these pubs started life as private houses where anyone who could brew ale could set him or herself up as a beer retailer. Most, however, were not licensed to sell spirits. This picture from the 1940s shows landlord David Proctor in the doorway behind Mrs Proctor, who has Joe Mills Snr in front of her. On the right are Philip Burgess and Miss Phyllis Burgess, while sitting on the step is Ernie Webb. (Albert Murphy)

Chapter Three

Work, Rest & Play

The junction of Horseley Road and Bridge Road, Toll End, with the cemetery and chapel in the background, 17 May 1941. This scene of devastation shows employees of the South Staffordshire Waterworks Company restoring water supplies following a German bombing raid earlier that day. The repair of this 20 inch cast-iron main took forty-eight hours and necessitated the closing down of Lichfield and Wood Green Pumping Stations while the work was carried out. (South Staffs Water)

The interior of the Wellington Tube Works, Great Bridge Street, *c.* 1931, showing the finishing shop for tubes over 2 inches in diameter. The manufacture of tubes on this site had been taking place since the early nineteenth century on land owned by Edward Elwell. The Wellington Tube Works was established in 1872 by Joseph Aird, who later purchased the Great Bridge Street Patent Tube Works, which had been operating on an adjacent site since 1861. The Asda supermarket now stands where this world-famous tube works once did. (Ian Bott)

The pattern shop of Brickhouse Foundry Ltd, Brickhouse Lane, Great Bridge, *c.* 1947. The man operating the bandsaw in the centre of the picture, cutting wooden blocks for use with recessed manhole covers, is Horace Carter, pattern maker, who retired in 1980 after an amazing fifty-three years of unbroken service. On the left an aluminium gully frame pattern is being repaired. Very little is known about the early history of these general ironfounders after they were established in Temple Street, West Bromwich in 1858. (Keith Cherrington)

A royal visit to Great Bridge by Prince Edward the Prince of Wales, seen here with the Chairman and Directors of the Wellington Tube Works, 11 May 1931. The Prince was on a tour of the Midlands, visiting some of the important firms in the area in his capacity as a Liaison Officer between the British Chamber of Commerce and our overseas markets. (T.J.H. Price)

Ratcliffs (Great Bridge) Ltd No. 1 Works, Eagle Lane, *c.* 1935. This interior view of the rolling mill shows, on the right of the picture, ½ inch brass strip leaving the machine after being reduced from an original thickness of 2–3 inches. The firm also produced copper strip to customers' individual requirements. (Frank Wardle)

Skilled workers in the cabinet shop of Kingfisher Ltd, Charles Street, Great Bridge, *c*. 1954. Many of the offices and schools in the Birmingham and Black Country areas would have been supplied with furniture manufactured by this company. Back row, first right: Gerald Madox. Front row, second right: Bert Pitt. Centre foreground: Ray Barnfield. (Joyce Stimpson)

Samuel Downing Little Mill, Richmond Ironworks, Brickhouse Lane, Great Bridge, 1913. Established in 1871, it had ten puddling furnaces, a primary rolling mill and two finishing mills. It is not known how long the company continued after the death of Samuel Downing in 1900, but in 1926 the site was purchased by the Midland Bright Drawn Steel & Engineering Company. The man wearing a collar and tie (centre back) is probably the manager as mill operators were not so well dressed. (Alan Price)

Employees of the Dial Works in Bagnall Street, Golds Hill, *c*. 1928. The firm originally made tubes for iron bedsteads before being sold to George Warwick, who eventually changed its name to The Warwick Rim, manufacturers of bicycle wheel rims and steering wheels for cars. At some point in the nineteenth century a section of Brickhouse Lane was renamed Dial Lane after this old established works. Back row, left to right: Gladys Shorthouse, Clara Hughes, Tom Cree, Harry Cree, Baden Fellows, Joan Warwick. Front row: Arthur Foster, Doris Cooper, Gladys Williamson, Mary Law, Elsie Skidmore, Mabel Hughes, Rose Rickuss. (Iris Warner)

The employees of Ratcliff & Ratcliff No. 1 Works, Eagle Lane, Great Bridge, photographed outside the weighbridge office at Frogs Meadow, *c*. 1920. The firm was run by two brothers, Martin and Bernard, who at that time specialised in the manufacture of steel tubes. The group, which includes the Works Manager Charlie Holden (second row, second right), is described on a sign to the left of the picture as 'The Awkward Squad'. (Albert Murphy)

Pictured here hop picking in the Worcestershire countryside are the Toon family from Horton Street, Great Bridge, *c.* 1948. Left to right: Sarah Toon, Jane Copper, Alice Reed, Tom Reed, Thomas Reed Jnr, Len Toon. (Lily Phillips)

The premises of William Thomas & Co., commercial body builders, at 161 Great Bridge Street, *c.* 1936. The firm was established in 1877 by wheelwright William Thomas who later called his premises the Wellington Carriage Works, a name which is perpetuated on the site of the original building. At some time in the 1930s the business was purchased and expanded by the Lavender family, one of whom, Lionel, on his return from the RAF in 1946 converted the front paint shop into a showroom selling bicycles, radios and later televisions. His brother Jim, together with one George Arthur, continued to run the motor body operation. By 1959 the firm had changed hands again when it was acquired by William Marshall, who six years later replaced the old building with a modern and much larger workshop unit. Between 1965 and 1975 the business continued to expand when additional property was obtained a short distance away at the rear of 111 Great Bridge Street. Today William's son Andrew manages the 123-year-old firm, which is now the oldest of its type in the West Bromwich area. Left to right: Tom Butler, Arthur Morris, Joseph Reynolds, Tom Morris. (Frank Reynolds)

Reynold's forge at the rear of 159 Great Bridge Street, *c.* 1945. Left to right: Louis Albrighton, 'Jimmy' the horse, Joseph Reynolds. As well as being a blacksmith specialising in the repair and rebuilding of carts, Joseph and his wife Elizabeth ran a general store from the same address. (Frank Reynolds)

The bacon factory, abattoir and general offices of W. Devis & Sons Ltd, 22 New Road, Great Bridge, *c.* 1945, formerly the Old Bush Inn run by licensee George Harrold. On the left of the picture is the private road leading to the abattoir, with on the right the cattle reception and marshalling yard. The business was established in a small shop at Great Bridge around 1880 by William Devis. By the time of his death in 1941 at the age of seventy-nine, he had built up a chain of almost twenty shops in the Tipton and Dudley areas. (Terry Scotland)

Volunteer firemen at the Great Bridge sub-station of the Tipton Auxiliary Fire Service pose for a photograph at their base, situated behind the premises of A.F. Welch Ltd in New Road, 1939. The Section Leader was Walter Linden, supported by Leading Fireman Percy Bryant and Deputy Leading Fireman Tom Parton. Back row, left to right: Percy Bryant, Austin Whitehouse, ? Mansell, -?-, David Jacks. Front row: Walter Linden, Tom Parton, Joe Cartwright, Ernie Hill. (Tom Parton)

Police Officers and 'Specials' line up for a photograph at the back of Greets Green police station in Whitehall Road, *c.* 1942. The station had a full-time complement of fifteen men and was a sub-section of West Bromwich. Back row, left to right: -?-, -?-, SC Nicholas, -?-, SC Arnold, PC Podmore, SC Ernie Rotten, -?-, SC Hopson, -?-, -?-. Middle row: -?-, MB Arthur Aston, -?-, SC Mason, -?-, SC J. Brisland, SC A. Kitely, -?-, -?-, -?-, -?-. Front row: PC Percival, Supt Nicholas, PC W. Share, -?-, Sgt Hopson, Sgt Horton, Sgt Wilcox, Sgt Rowbotham, -?-, SC Bird, -?-. (Doreen Markham)

Great Bridge ARP (Air Raid Precautions) team, July 1941. In April 1937 a national Air Raid Wardens Service was created and within twelve months it had some 200,000 recruits. Another 500,000 people enrolled during the 'Munich crisis' of 1938 when trench shelters were dug in public parks. Back row, third from left: Cliff Warren; Middle row, Second from left: Alf Gilson. (Philip Evans)

Members of the Great Bridge fire watching squad of 1943. Following German bombing raids at the outbreak of the Second World War, directives were issued for the introduction of compulsory fire watching with effect from 31 December 1940. Back row, left to right: J. Hodgetts, E. Ingram, Cliff Warren, Charlie Warren. Front row: ? Smith, Arthur Winsper, ? Bratby. (Philip Evans)

Employees of Braithwaite & Co., Structural Engineers, Ryder Street, Great Bridge, are pictured here in 1951 after being called up for national service in the RAF. On the extreme left of the group in the front row is Ron Downes. Right up to the late 1950s national service was compulsory for all young men reaching the age of eighteen, but if an indentured apprenticeship was being served it could be deferred to twenty-one, as was the case with these lads. (Ian Downes)

The Braithwaite and Wellington Tube Works Division of the Home Guard behind the Drill Hall at Carters Green, West Bromwich, *c.* 1940. Employees of these two Great Bridge firms who were on essential war work or were too old for national service had volunteered to join this force and undertake training at camp in their spare time. Captain Harry Cotterill, in the peaked cap, was the Commander, while Private Bob Stokes is pictured in the second row from the back, third from the left. (Danny Stokes)

Members of the White Swan (Vernon Street) marching jazz band pictured on 'The Lily' at Greets Green, *c.* 1930. In the background is a section of the Stour Valley railway line between Albion and Dudley Port stations. On the right, with a collecting box, is Mrs Green and behind her, wearing a headband, is May Jones. First line on the right, third from the front: Jack Ramsell. Front row, first left: Harry Newey, with Beattie Pitt on his right. (Brenda Mackay)

An outing from the Beehive, Charles Street, Great Bridge to Evesham, 1920. The pub's landlord at the time was George 'Monkey' Jackson, who held the licence from around 1910 until 1952. Standing in front of the charabanc is William Webley, Minister of the nearby Great Bridge Street Primitive Methodist chapel, while behind the vehicle's windscreen, fourth from the left, is Harold Markham. (Doreen Boucher)

St Peter's church Mother's Meeting outing to the seaside, in Whitehall Road before departure, 1920. This annual event, which was always very popular, was organised by Captain Welch from the nearby Church Army Social Centre. Standing in front of the coach are, from left to right: the Revd Frank Smith, Vicar; the Revd F.W. Mellor, Curate; Captain Welch. (Pat Redrup)

Seven of Allsopp's Vanguard Super Coaches are lined up here in Henry Street, Great Bridge, waiting to take the employees of Braithwaite Engineering Co on their annual trip, July 1929. In later years this section of Henry Street was totally consumed by Braithwaite's, making it impossible for the general public to travel through. (Harry Allsopp)

A 'Dickie Horton's' coach stands by waiting to take members of St Peter's church, Whitehall Road, on a trip to Blackpool, late 1940s. Horton's Coaches were based in Whitgreave Street, Greets Green and the driver seen here on the left is Dickie himself, with Captain Allway close by. Among the group on the right of the picture are Brenda Woodbine, Freda Turner, Emily Tonks, Ike Faulkener and Jean Barnett. (Lily Phillips)

A Sunday morning breakfast outing from the Plough & Harrow pub, William Street, Great Bridge, *c.* 1963. These 'men only' drinking trips were a great Black Country tradition in the old days. Among those on the front row are: Fred Glover, Luke Dunne, Tom Bagley, Cyril Jones, Arthur Simms, George Yates, Tom Simpson, Bernard Morris and Jack Yates. Among the back row are: Jack Davis, Jack Read, Jack Grainger, Gordon Lockley; Tom Ore, Ray Partridge, John Edwards, Arthur Wood, Cyril Jones (licensee), Reg Shaw, Richard Round and Sam Merchant. Sitting in the coach is Freddy Merchant. (Gordon Lockley)

Members of Great Bridge Methodist Youth Club congregate outside Fisher Street Schools in preparation for their trip to Blackpool, *c.* 1956. The coach, which was driven by Bob Barlow, was on hire from Hill's of West Bromwich. Among those pictured are Bob and Lillian Stokes; Barry Stokes, Sheila Cash, Sheila Jones, Danny Stokes, John Crutchley, George Bullock and George Roper. (Danny Stokes)

The Committee of the Great Bridge Methodist Youth Club at Fisher Street Schools, *c.* 1956. Back row, left to right: Clive Weigh, Danny Stokes, George Roper, Brian Bull, John Lawley. Front row: Freda Roberts, Sheila Jones, -?-, -?-, Betty Gibbs, Doreen ?. (Danny Stokes)

One of the classrooms at Fisher Street Schools being used by the Youth Club of Great Bridge Methodists to play various games such as snooker, table tennis and draughts, *c.* 1956. The club was established in 1955 by Danny Stokes and Freddy Middleton and ran until 1958, when National Service commitments drastically reduced the numbers. At its peak the club had a membership of around 100 teenagers. (Danny Stokes)

The Great Bridge Methodist Youth Club rocking and rolling the night away at Fisher Street Schools, playing hit records borrowed from a local radio shop, *c.* 1956. The tall lad at the back in charge of the music is John Lawley, the club's DJ. Today this would be called a 'disco', but back then the word had not been invented. (Danny Stokes)

A VE Day children's party being held in the yard behind the Plough & Harrow in William Street, Great Bridge, 8 May 1945. The lady on the left nearest the camera holding a young child is Edith Botfield, while at the end of the table is Ruth Eaton dressed as 'Monty'. The young lady standing with her arms folded on the middle right of the picture is Janet Price. (Peter Coley)

The children pictured here on 8 May 1945 are celebrating the end of the Second World War at a VE Day party being held in a yard behind shops numbered 55 to 61 Great Bridge, near to where the new market hall now stands. Among those in the second row are Alf Rayers and Brian Rayers; in the front row, third from right, is Danny Stokes; fourth from right is Freddy Middleton. (Danny Stokes)

A Queen Elizabeth II coronation party for children, at the rear of the Plough & Harrow pub, William Street, Great Bridge, 2 June 1953. Among the many pictured here are Jim Price, George Price, Michael Hitch, John Morris, Rose Morris, Maud Dyas, Tom Withington, Tommy Horton, Les Baker, Mary Baker, Edna Kendrick, Jean Fletcher, Olive Fletcher, Susan Fletcher, Janet Fletcher, Evelyn Fletcher, Francis Hill, Terry Slater and Sheila Slater. (Olive Peters)

Residents in and around Ballfields, Great Bridge, celebrate the coronation of Queen Elizabeth II, 2 June 1953. Towering over Tame Road in the background is the chimney-stack of Hadley's Brickworks on what is now Sheepwash Lane Urban Park. Among those pictured are John Edwards, Mrs Jeavons, Mark Hawthorn, Mrs Guest, Valerie Edwards, Pat Wilkes, June Davies, Colin Davies, Carol Wilkes, Edna Reed, Mrs Edmunds, Valerie Smith, Mrs Hawthorn, Eileen Davies, Tom Browning, Bill Edwards, Maureen Davies, Mrs Rutter, Mrs Browning and Mrs Davies. (Val Harris)

Children and parents enjoy a party at the Wagon & Horses Hotel, Great Bridge, to celebrate the coronation of Queen Elizabeth II, 2 June 1953. Landlord John Webb and his wife Margaret had put on a magnificent spread and each child was given a suitably decorated cup, saucer and plate. Carol and Anthony Hughes, whose father Howard Hughes was licensee of the Lion from 1947 to 1953, are seated towards the top of the table on the right of the picture. (Carol Osborne)

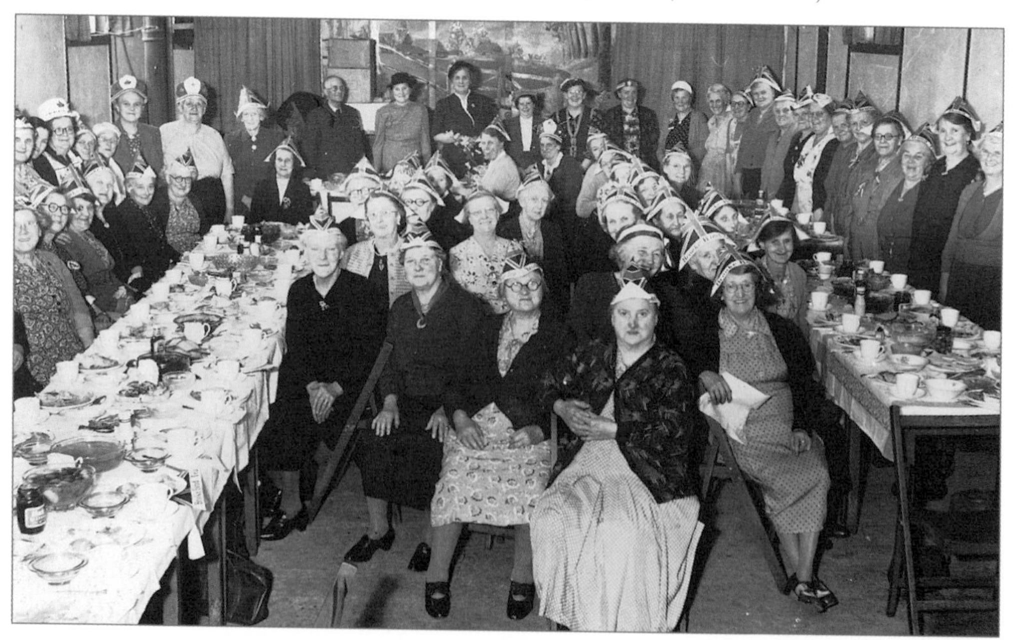

St Peter's church Mothers' Meeting coronation party in the Mission Hall, which was situated on the corner of Farley Street and Whitehall Road, June 1953. The event was organised by Captain Willoughby Allway and his wife, who are both pictured on the left of the top table. Next to Mrs Allway is the local doctor's wife Mrs Spring. The hall was at one time a venue for dancing and was known in the area as the 'Stampede'. (David Allway)

Children in fancy dress outside 14 Hope Road, Great Bridge, during the Queen Elizabeth II Silver Jubilee celebrations of 1977. Among those in the photograph, from left to right, are Katie Baker, Mark Buckley (the Wizard), Douglas Shipley and Martin Powell. On the extreme right is John Powell (Jack of Hearts). (Mary Law)

Neighbours from the Sheepwash Lane area of Great Bridge interrupt their King George VI coronation celebrations to pose for a photograph, May 1937. Included in the back row are Bill Bennett, Ann Wright, Eddie Phillips, Ann Connor, Daisy Toon, Joan Phillips, Dave Freeman, Hannah Phillips, Winnie Freeman and Rose Stott. Front row: -?-, Ada Dickinson, May Bennett, May Stimpson, -?-, -?-, Alice Toon, Irene Stott. (Elizabeth Bignell)

Elwell Street, Great Bridge, coronation fancy dress competition, 2 June 1953, a wonderful example of the atmosphere prevailing at the time. The smiling faces here include Linda Markham, Brian Edmunds, Gloria Sansome, Ann Stamps, Trevor Jinks, Ann Burns, Margaret Markham, Jean Rackham, Margaret Ingram, Jennifer Evans, John Burns and Jacky Best. (Hilda Palmer)

Elwell Street, Great Bridge, coronation day, 2 June 1953. This picture shows track events being held on the Wellington Tube Works sports ground prior to the children's party, which had to be switched to Braithwaite's canteen because of inclement weather. Pictured on the left are Linda Markham, Liza Shenstone, Arthur Capewell and Cecil Palmer. In the centre with a pram is Elsie Aston. On the right are Ann Burns, Margaret Markham, Gillian Evans and Marilyn Taylor. (John Palmer)

'Our Gang' pictured on the 'top field', Richmond Street, Great Bridge, *c.* 1953. Children from around the area of Brickhouse Lane and Elwell Street had for years used this open field to engage in various sporting activities, and during the severe winter of 1947 scores of people could be seen here digging for coal. Most of the lads pictured here later formed a football team called Elwell Eagles. Back row, left to right: John Crutchley, Brian Shenstone, John Palmer, Derek Markham, John Fereday. Front row: Michael Pace, Laurence Markham, John Martin, George Bullock. (Michael Pace)

The first works outing from the Triplex Foundry, Toll End Road to Worcester, August 1920. The firm was established in 1918 by Charles Horrell, who is pictured on the back row, eighth from the left. After the firm moved from Toll End Road to Upper Church Lane in 1936, the site was taken over by the baby carriage manufacturer Tan Sad. Some of the people in this photograph were founder employees, such as Samuel Price, back row, first left. (T.J.H. Price)

The interior of the St Peter's Church Army Social Centre, Greets Green, *c.* 1933. Opened in October 1919 and staffed by its first resident, Captain Peever, it provided leisure facilities and a meeting point not only for the unemployed of the area but also men returning from the war. Three captains followed in quick succession, Robinson, Welch and Gibbs, until in 1926 Captain and Mrs Willoughby Allway arrived, and together they ministered to the local people for the next twenty-seven years. After a short period under Captain Booth the centre finally closed in 1957. Captain and Mrs Allway are pictured second and third from the left next to the Mayor of West Bromwich, C.B. Adams. Seventh from the right, holding a cup, is Sam Harper. (David Allway)

Greets Green Liberal Club, Whitehall Road, Annual General Meeting, 13 May 1920. Built in 1911, the club was formed by local businessmen, one of whom was Councillor John Bell. He is pictured seated on the floor, front row, second from the left with a moustache. Also in the group, behind the cup on the billiard table, is professional football player Tom Bowen Snr. (Philip Evans)

The bandstand, Farley Park, Greets Green, *c.* 1903. On the left of the picture are St Peter's church and schoolrooms, with on the right the park-keeper's lodge. The park was presented to the Borough of West Bromwich by Great Bridge-born Reuben Farley in 1891. It was extended by 3½ acres in 1955 to provide three hard surface tennis courts and a general play area for children. (T.J.H. Price)

The dolls' hospital at William Reynold's hairdressing and newsagent's shop, 33 Market Place, Great Bridge, *c.* 1955. This repair facility, established in 1910 by William himself, was at the time one of the few of its kind operating in the Black Country area. Pictured here in the 'surgery' engaged in remedial work are, from left to right, William Reynolds, Hazel Reynolds and Walter Reynolds. (Walter Reynolds)

Although of poor quality this early photograph, showing the Palace Cinema, Great Bridge, under construction in about 1910, is worth including, as it is the only photograph known to exist. Built on the site of an old eighteenth-century tollhouse, at the corner of Slater Street, the Palace was first licensed by the West Bromwich Borough Council in November 1912. It was owned by a group of gentlemen by the names of Mr Spittle, Mr Marston, Mr Evans, Mr Dixon and Mr E.J. (Ted) Crinnian, who also ran it on a day to day basis. In 1933, two years after the introduction of 'talkies', the cinema was purchased by Cyril Joseph and Partners, under the name of Storer Pictures, who ran it until 1958 when it was sold to Vincent Wareing. It was he who put up the poster outside proclaiming 'bring your Alice to our Palace'. Sadly the Palace closed on 16 April 1960 with the film *Valley of Fury*, starring Victor Mature. Pictured on the front of the balcony above the foyer, from left to right, are Tom Spittle, Mary Spittle and Ted Crinnian. (John Barker)

The Victoria Palace Cinema, Railway Street, Horseley Heath, August 1968. Built originally as a Primitive Methodist chapel in 1859, it became a cinema in 1912 under the ownership of Tipton Councillor William Wooley Doughty JP. During the silent film era one of the many pianists was Leslie Taff, who in 1935 became the organist at the Tower Cinema, West Bromwich. The Victoria Palace closed around 1955 and then in 1960 became a storage facility for the firm of Horseley Bridge & Thomas Piggott. (Alan Price)

Players and officials of Horseley Bridge FC, members of the Birmingham Works League, pictured on the Triplex Sports Ground in Horseley Road, Great Bridge, *c.* 1952. Back row, left to right: ? Hudson, Arthur Wall, ? Cooper, William Hudson, -?-, Brian Kingston, Geoff Brookes, Albert Simmons, -?-. Front row: Harold Benton, -?-, Peter Lewis, ? Turvey, -?-. (Geoff Brookes)

Members of the Church Army Social football team with the West Bromwich League's Albion Shield, 1948/9 season. Back row, left to right: Captain Allway, Sid Stevens, Ken Hodgkisson, Billy Hunt, Tommy Harper, John Fox, Sam Merchant, Harry Bird, Jackie Goodwin, Ray Wyant, Arthur Hartshorne. Front row: Norman Stevens, Bernard Morris, Eddie Gill, Derek Hodgkisson, Freddy Marsh. (Ken Hodgkisson)

Elwell Eagles from Elwell Street, Great Bridge, are pictured here before playing their first ever match in the Handsworth Junior League, 1958. The track-suited player on the right of the picture, Brian Edmunds, eventually went on to play for Halesowen Town. Back row, left to right: John Palmer, Louis Albrighton, Frank Fryer, John Wood, Jim Powell, Ron Hall, Derek Markham, Brian Edmunds. Front row: Michael Kennett, Arthur Crutchley, Terry Price, Michael Pace; Keith Stubbs. (T.J.H. Price)

Elwell FC, Great Bridge, 1961. After merging with local rivals, Newtown United, the club at last tasted success by winning both the Handsworth Cup and the T.R. Fardell Cup in the 1960/1 season. Three years later they won the Premier Division of the Handsworth League before entering the Warwickshire & West Midlands Football Alliance in 1964. Back row, left to right: Billy Harris, Harry Grice, Ken Hunter, John Collins, Reg Price, Peter O'Dea. Front row: Brian Cadd, Michael Kellas, Wilf Stokes, Roy Law, Harry Rose. (T.J.H. Price)

Newtown United, Great Bridge on 'Tommy Wright's Fields', 1958. The team, which was made up of lads from the local Newtown housing estate, played in the Tipton League for just one season before eventually merging with Elwell FC. Back row, left to right: Wilf Stokes; Brian Aston, Brian Ruston, Ken Hunter, Michael Wherton, Alan Bratt, Harry Grice. Front row: Leslie Withers, Roy Stanton, John Nicholls, Barry Morris, John Foster, Geoff May. (Wilf Stokes)

Toll End Juniors at the rear of the Shakespeare Pub, Bridge Road, after winning the West Bromwich League Cup in the 1920/1 season. The team, most of whom had seen service in the First World War, were noted for being physically tough. They later merged with Toll End Wesley. Back row, left to right: Joe Deakin, Jack Gibbs, Ben Brinsdon, Fred Pyatt, Jack Gray, Joe Foster, Dan Deakin. Middle row: Isiah Cash, 'Cock' Handley, Ben Smitherman. Front row: Arthur Ward, John Price, Tom Gibbs, Ike Brockston, Herbert Roper. (T.J.H. Price)

Queens Head FC, Great Bridge, also known as 'Tommy Wright's', 1947/8. After beating Gower OB in the final, they are pictured here outside the Queen's Head in Horton Street with the Handsworth League's Lewis Cup. Back row, left to right: Bert Clark (licensee), Arthur May, Joe Hichinbottom, Alf Long, Walter Plested, Sid Davies, Arthur Dudfield, Horace Silwood, Arthur Jones, 'Dot' Boughton. Front row: Bill Ruston, Len Walker, Peter Reed, Jess Bowen, Walter Silwood. (Walter Silwood)

Queen's Head Reserves FC, Great Bridge, 1934. Even 'Tommy Wright's' reserve team was a formidable outfit, winning both the Handsworth League Shield and Cup during the 1933/4 season. There were teams playing for this public house as far back as the early 1920s, when Joe Dyke was a member of the selection committee. The trainer on the extreme left, back row, is Thomas Phillips, while the goalkeeper, fourth from right, is Joe Botfield. (Lily Phillips)

Pictured receiving the Britannia Cup from West Bromwich Albion Secretary Alan Everiss at The Hawthorns is Greets Green Prims captain Harry Bird, *c.* 1964. This well-known team from the Whitehall Road Primitive Methodist chapel had just beaten Corser Street Prims in the Smethwick League's equivalent of the Albion Shield. Left to right: Sid Day, Stan Bates, Billy Richards, Alan Parkes, Alan Everiss, Arthur Devaney, John Ainge, Harry Bird, Billy Todd, David Broad, Harry Lister, Arthur Biston, David Nightingale (mascot), Philip Nightingale, David Nightingale Snr. (Joan Devaney)

Greets Green Prims Youth FC, 1955. Based at the Primitive Methodist chapel in Greets Green, 'The Prims' were one of the best known and most successful teams in the Black Country. The team pictured here were winners of the Smethwick League Division 5 in the 1954/5 season. Back row, left to right: David Dyke, Terry Talbot, Ron Bates, Roy Stearn, Tony Welch, Jimmy Cox, Stan Downing, Arthur Brown, Alan Griffiths, Ernie Ainge, Brian Harley, Jack Dyke. Front row: Trevor Woolley, Colin Whitehouse, Terry Pottinger, Derek Smith, Derek Bradley, Geoff Gill. Seated on the grass: Graham Dyke, John Ainge. (David Dyke)

Great Bridge Celtic, seen here on Palethorpes ground around 1953, were based at the Old Crown in Sheepwash Lane and played their football in the Tipton League. Back row, left to right: Len Stevens (referee), -?-, George Pritchard, Leslie Jones, Ray Earpe, John Wherton, -?-, -?-, -?-, Len Jones (manager). Front row: Henry Witney, -?-, -?-, Sam Smith, Bob Ruston, -?-. (Lily Phillips)

Members of the Great Bridge Juniors Football Team, who in 1948 were the Tipton Boys League champions and cup winners. Their home pitch was situated to the rear of the Royal Oak pub in Whitehall Road, with changing facilities at the old St Peter's church schoolrooms. Back row, left to right: Frank Turner, Freddy Bellingham, Colin Smith, David Almark, Colin Higginson, Mr Higginson (manager), George Pritchard. Front row: Henry Bayliss, Frank Walters, Arthur Horton, Len Whitehouse, Gilbert Boxley. (George Pritchard)

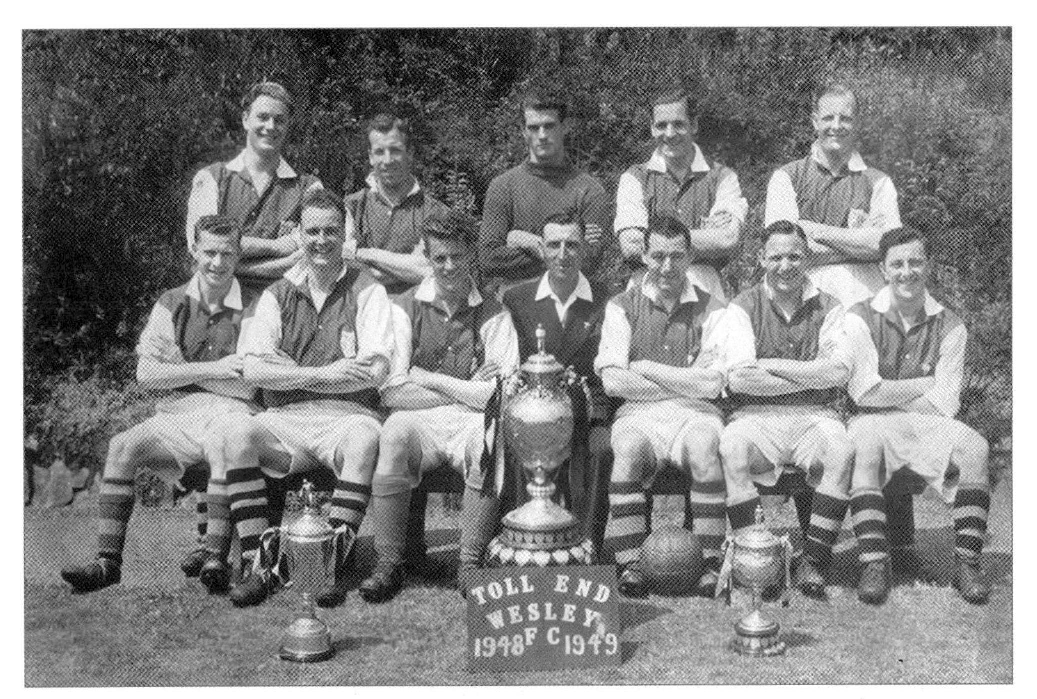

Possibly the oldest established amateur football team in Britain, with a history going back to at least 1905, the mighty Toll End Wesley is pictured here in 1949. Champions of the Wolverhampton Amateur League Division I, the team also won the League Cup, Dudley Guest Hospital Cup and the Wednesbury Charity Cup. Back row, left to right: Bob Ashley, Reg Kramier, Jim Plaza, Cyril Payton, Jacky Bache. Front row: Doug Millington, Jimmy Darling, William ('Curly') Bull, Walter Walker, Dennis Baker, Sammy Page, Jack Gray. (Jack Gray)

Displaying their Inter-Branch and Birmingham Works League Division 2 trophies in 1961 is the victorious cricket team of Braithwaite & Co., Ryder Street, Great Bridge, 1961. On the front row, extreme right, is Fred Bradley. This world-famous firm of structural engineers, like so many others in the Black Country, actively encouraged its employees to participate in cricket and football. (Ian Downes)

Greets Green Liberal Club snooker team outside their premises in Whitehall Road after winning Division I of the West Bromwich League, *c.* 1947. Back row, left to right: Albert Rotten, -?-, Arthur Parsons, Bill Scarlett. Front row: Harry Birch, George Ward, Charles Bailey. (George Ward)

Salem Guild Billiards Club, Sheepwash Lane, Great Bridge, 1915. The team pictured here had won the Tipton Church League and contained a number of prominent businessmen. Among those in the back row are, first left, William Bagnall; second left, John Richardson; and extreme right Isaac Parkes. Front row, fourth from the left, is Joe Grinsill, and fifth from the left is Billy Jones, who in 1932 built the church hall. (Annie Ball)

Tom Parton of Webb Road, Toll End, displays the 'Best in Show' trophy won by his whippet Sylvia at the Midlands Area Dog Show, which was held at the Wagon & Horses Hotel, Great Bridge in 1938. Events such as this, including wrestling matches, were frequently hosted at this popular venue by landlord George Reaney. In later years Tom was to become a licensee himself at a number of pubs in the area, before finally retiring in 1976 after six years in charge of the Limerick in Great Bridge Market Place. (Tom Parton)

The Church Army Social Centre, Whitehall Road, Greets Green, table tennis team, *c.* 1942. Playing in Division I of the West Bromwich League, this team won every competition they entered, with two of their players receiving representative honours. Back row, left to right: Jess Bowen, Albert Plested, Sam Dudfield, Captain Allway, George Millward, Horace Cross. Front row: Tommy Baker, Jack Carter, Tommy Bowen. (Ken Hodgkisson)

Greets Green Bowling Club, Farley Park, based at the Rose & Crown in Cape Street, *c*. 1935. Back row, left to right: -?-, Bert Capewell, Albert Bird, George Hickman, -?-, -?-, Arthur Shelly, Billy Clifton, Ted Reynolds. Middle row: -?-, Evan Griffiths, Tom Fathers, Tom Arnold, ? Bearde, Isiah Brown, -?-, -?-, Gerald Haddock, Jack Edwards. Front row: -?-, John Davies, -?-, -?-, Bill Gamble, -?-, -?-, Ernie Simms, -?-, -?-, Tom Williams, Tom Cook. (George Ward)

The Stork Inn Bowling Club, Great Bridge, *c*. 1916. This was one of the few pubs in the Great Bridge area that had its own first-class bowling green, and licensee Frederick Parker, pictured seated on the left in shirtsleeves, was justifiably proud of it. On the front row second from the right is Charles Swift Snr with his son, also Charles, seated in the second row on the extreme left. (Chas Swift)

CHAPTER FOUR

LOCAL PERSONALITIES

Ken Hodgkisson with the Walsall FC Player of the Season award for 1962/3, after receiving the highest number of votes ever cast by the Supporters Club. He was instrumental in Walsall winning the Fourth Division Championship in 1960 and played an important part in their rise to the Second Division the year after. In 1966, after 352 appearances and 60 goals covering 11 years, Ken left the 'Saddlers' for non-league football with Worcester City and Dudley Town. (Ken Hodgkisson)

Joshua Churchman JP, who in 1966 became the first Mayor of the new County Borough of West Bromwich, which included Tipton and Wednesbury. Born in 1922 in Whitehall Road, he attended St Peter's and Greets Green Junior Schools, before finishing his education at the George Salter School at the age of fourteen. After moving to Tipton and joining the local Labour Party in 1948, he fought two elections and first won a seat on the Council in 1951 representing the Horseley Heath Ward. During the municipal year 1964–5 he was Deputy Mayor under Councillor W.E. Drew, and by the time Tipton Borough Council was defunct he had served on every committee, including Chairman of those dealing with libraries, housing and road safety. After a long and distinguished career he retired from public service in 1973. (Joshua Churchman)

Alderman William Horace Gladstone Hirons, elected Mayor of Tipton during the municipal year of 1957. Born in Charles Street, Great Bridge, in 1901, he attended Fisher Street Schools where he completed his education at the age of thirteen. Elected as a member of the Tipton Borough Council in 1946, and Alderman in 1951, he completed twenty years' service when Tipton amalgamated with West Bromwich in 1966. In recognition of his long and valuable service, on 19 May 1970 the Council conferred on him the Freedom of the County Borough of West Bromwich. According to tradition he was presented with a copy of the Resolution of Council illuminated and engrossed on vellum, and contained within a casket of Japanese oak bearing a carved reproduction of the Tipton Mace. He died two years later in 1972. (Gordon Hirons)

Alderman Reuben Farley JP, the first and five times Mayor of West Bromwich between 1882 and 1895, was born in Whitehall Road, Newtown, Great Bridge, on 27 January 1826. On leaving school he became an apprentice mining surveyor, and by 1847 had acquired and developed the Dunkirk Colliery. He remained single until the age of forty but afterwards married three times, first to Hannah Duce, second to Elizabeth Haines and thirdly to a Miss Fellows with whom he had five children. In 1875 he erected the Farley Fountain in Dartmouth Square, West Bromwich in memory of his mother Elizabeth, gave Farley Park to the town in 1891 and in 1898, after its restoration, presented the Oak House to the West Bromwich Corporation for use as a museum. On 20 April 1896, in recognition of his outstanding service and munificent gifts to the town, he had the distinction of being made the first Freeman of West Bromwich. In 1897 a magnificent clock tower was erected at Carters Green in his honour. He died two years later on 11 March 1899 at the age of seventy-three. (Ian Bott)

The actor Raymond Mason was born on 17 April 1924 in Horseley Heath, Great Bridge. His parents, George and Elizabeth, ran two shops, a confectioner's and a tobacconist's, while on the opposite side of the road his uncle, Evan Mason, and his wife ran a fish and chip shop. After living for a short while in Darlaston and then Tettenhall he moved to London in 1935, where he became a pupil and chorister at the London Choir School in Camberwell. In 1947, after five years in the RAF, he obtained a Sir Alexander Korda Scholarship to RADA where he studied until 1949. There followed ten years of repertory until eventually he became involved in television, his first appearance being in a Midland series called *The Wright People*, live from Aston TV Studios. After graduating to *Emergency Ward 10* he went on to appear in *Crossroads*, playing five different characters over its run. He also played Reg Palmer in the serial *Muck and Brass*. After appearing in hundreds of film, television and theatre productions, Raymond, a proud family man, is still working after fifty years in the profession. (Raymond Mason)

Thomas George Bowen – a professional football player with Walsall, Wolves and Coventry – was born on 16 January 1900 in Grout Street and educated at Greets Green Junior School. After leaving school he played for Bush Rangers before having a brief spell as an amateur with Birmingham City in 1920. A year later in July 1921 he signed professional forms for Walsall where he spent three seasons at inside forward, scoring seventeen goals in eighty-one appearances. His next move, in March 1924, took him to Wolves with Ben Timmins in a combined deal worth just £130. In September 1925 he gained representative honours when appearing for a Birmingham & District team against an FA eleven. After scoring twenty-four goals in ninety-four appearances for Wolves he was transferred to Coventry City, where he stayed for the next two years. Tommy left league football in August 1930 to play for Kidderminster Harriers where, in 1933, he retired from the game. (Jess Bowen)

Thomas ('Toddy') Bowen – a professional football player with West Bromwich Albion, Newport County and Walsall. Son of Thomas George Bowen and brother of Reg, Tommy was born in Grout Street in August 1924 and attended Greets Green Junior and George Salter Schools. In August 1945 he became a professional when he signed for his home town club West Bromwich Albion but later moved away to join Newport County in July 1946. Known for his speed on the right wing, he stayed with the Welsh club for four years, scoring six goals in thirty-seven league games. Ater longing for a return to the Midlands he eventually signed for Walsall on 30 June 1950, where he spent three happy years, scoring seven goals in ninety-seven appearances. Tommy retired from league football in May 1953. (Geoff Allman)

Reg Bowen was a professional football player with Hereford United. Brother to 'Toddy' and son of Thomas George Bowen, Reg was born in Grout Street in 1928 and also educated at Greets Green Junior and George Salter schools. In 1942 he joined the Hill Top Boys Brigade where he met another promising football player, Jimmy Dudley. During the war years Reg played for Toll End Wesley, Church Army Social and made guest appearances for West Bromwich Albion's youth team who tried to sign him in 1945. In 1949, after completing his national service, Reg became a professional with Hereford United where he remained for thirteen years. Noted for his speed on the right wing he scored over 100 goals in more than 500 appearances for the club. In 1962 Reg began his move back to the Midlands by signing first for Bromsgrove Rovers and then in 1964 for Halesowen Town. Reg retired from the game in 1965. (Reg Bowen)

Ken Hodgkisson – professional football player with West Bromwich Albion and Walsall. Born in March 1933 in Grout Street, Ken attended Greets Green Junior and George Salter Schools. After playing for Newtown Rangers and the Church Army Social he signed professional forms for West Bromwich Albion in 1949, making his debut at Villa Park in April 1953 in front of 49,500 fans. Ken was an early member of that glorious 1953/4 side, playing at inside right in the first five matches of Albion's undefeated start to the season. After twenty-one first team appearances and four goals he was transferred to Walsall in December 1955 for £1,600. Ken returned to the Albion as a coach in 1975, teaming up with an old Walsall colleague, Albert McPherson. In 1981 Ken was promoted to youth team manager at the Hawthorns, a position he held until 1983. After scouting for several clubs, including Albion and Derby County, he retired in 1987. (Ken Hodgkisson)

Bill Richardson – professional football player with West Bromwich Albion and Swindon Town. Born in February 1908 in Whitehall Road and brother of Sammy, Bill was educated at Greets Green Junior School. After leaving at the age of fourteen he turned out for Greets Green Prims and Great Bridge Celtic before joining West Bromwich Albion as a professional in November 1926. He made his debut in a 1–1 draw away at Middlesbrough on 1 December 1928 and afterwards was rarely out of the team. In fact, between 1928 and 1937 Albion played a total of 347 league matches and Bill appeared in 319 of them, mostly at centre half where his dominance in the air was outstanding. He was also a member of that fabulous cup and promotion winning team of 1930/1, a unique double which has never been emulated by any other club. Bill played a total of 352 games for the 'Baggies' before moving to Swindon Town in May 1937. After playing non-league football for Dudley Town and Vono Sports, he retired in 1941. (Tony Matthews)

Sammy Richardson – professional football player with West Bromwich Albion, Newport County and Aldershot. Born in 1892 in Whitehall Road, Sammy attended Greets Green Junior School until the age of thirteen. Periods with Greets Green Prims, Great Bridge Juniors and Great Bridge Celtic followed before he signed professional forms for West Bromwich Albion in 1913. A physically strong wing half who was biting in the tackle, he was a key member of Albion's record breaking 1919/20 league championship-winning side who became the first team to score over 100 goals in a season. In 1921 he represented both the FA and the Football League at international level. Brother of Bill Richardson, Albion's centre half, Sammy played in over 200 games until in August 1927 he was transferred to Newport County. After a spell with Aldershot Sammy retired in 1931. (Tony Matthews)

Jacky Mann – professional football player with West Bromwich Albion, Newport County and Walsall. Born in 1891 in Brickhouse Lane, Great Bridge, and educated at Fisher Street School, Jacky played for Great Bridge Celtic, Hurst Hill Rovers and Bilston United before joining West Bromwich Albion on professional terms in April 1912. He spent seven seasons at The Hawthorns although four of those campaigns were lost because of the First World War. A hard working centre forward with a tremendous shot, he made only two first team appearances for the Albion, although he did play in ten unclassified wartime matches scoring eight goals, including a hat-trick in a 5–1 win over Aston Villa in December 1916. In July 1919 he was transferred to Newport County for £195 and the following year moved again, this time to Walsall. He was plagued by injuries, however, and after scoring just six goals in thirty-one outings for the 'Saddlers' he left the club for non-league soccer in May 1921. Jacky retired from playing just four years later. (Tony Matthews)

Jack Hughes – professional football player with Walsall FC – was born in September 1929 in Pikehelve Street and educated at Golds Hill and All Saints Schools. After playing for Stone Cross Star in the Handsworth League he signed amateur forms for West Bromwich Albion, but National Service prevented any further progress. On leaving the army Jack played for Golden Lion FC, Stone Cross and again joined the 'Albion' as an amateur before eventually signing professional forms for Walsall in May 1950. He was a versatile forward, able to play in any position but preferred the inside left berth where he was able to display his dribbling and scheming abilities to the full. He remained with the 'Saddlers' for three seasons, appearing in forty-four league games and scoring ten goals. Jack's best season was in 1950/1, when after scoring on his debut against Port Vale he netted five times in eighteen league games. He went on to play for Worcester City, Stourbridge and Evesham United before retiring in 1962. (Iris Warner)

Albert H. Hodson in his corn and seed shop at 5 and 6 New Road, Great Bridge, *c.* 1958. He was born at 3 Slater Street in 1910 and educated at Fisher Street and West Bromwich Grammar Schools. He served with distinction during the Second World War with the 8th Army (the Desert Rats), seeing action in Tobruk and El-Alamein. During the 1950s he expanded the business by acquiring two more shops at Wednesbury and Willenhall. In May 1961 he was elected to represent the Horseley Heath Ward on the Tipton Borough Council. He died in 1975, aged sixty-five. (Philip Evans)

Great Bridge confectioners and ice cream manufacturers Peter and Anita Bonaccorsi are pictured here with Peter's father and mother, Giuseppe and Alma, at the christening of their daughter Cynthia in 1926. Also in the photograph with Cynthia, who was born above the shop at 120 New Road, are Peter's aunt (standing centre), his brothers and sisters and his two year old son John. Back row, left to right: Hilda, Maurizio (George), Mariana, Marcello (Mark), Mary. Front row: Peter, Giuseppe (Joseph), John, Alma, Cynthia, Anita. (Cynthia Bonaccorsi)

CHAPTER FIVE

CHAPEL, CHURCH & SCHOOL

St Paul's church, Golds Hill Sunday School Anniversary parade, June 1951. Displaying their new banner in Bagnall Street during the Sunday School processions are, left to right, Walter Sharman, William Andrews, -?- and Joe Williams. The Vicar at the time was the Revd B.M. Rees, who reported that a total of £88 11*s* 5*d* had been raised from the anniversary. (Fred Dyson)

Great Bridge Street Primitive Methodist Sunday School Anniversary, *c.* 1945. Built in 1883 at a cost of £800 and seating 200 people, the chapel was at first in the Queen Street West Bromwich Circuit. Among the children pictured are, back row, left to right: Jim Harris, John Gough, Terry Simms; middle row, fourth from left: Janet Downing; Nellie Harris, Doris Maull, Audrey Downing, front row fifth from right: Ann Burns. (Audrey Downing)

Salem Congregational church, Sheepwash Lane, Great Bridge, Sunday School Anniversary, *c.* 1955. Among those on the platform are, back row third from left: Manny Wright; second row, fifth from left: Iris Day; seventh from left: Dora Day. The organist was Mr Goode, and in the fourth row is choirmaster Horace Parkes. (Iris Rich)

Children outside the Primitive Methodist chapel in Great Bridge Street during the Sunday School Anniversary celebrations of *c.* 1948, with Superintendent Sam Wall on the left. Back row, first on the right: Harold Yates; third from the right, Janet Downing. Third row, left to right: Sheila Capewell, Maurice Knight, Gary Albrighton, -?-, Audrey Downing, Doris Maull, Joan Clark, Clive Hickinbottom, John Spink (superintendent), Pam Coley. Second row: -?-, Linda Markham, Dorothy Parsons, Shirley Bromley, Ann Burns. Front row, first on left: John Palmer. (John Palmer)

Salem chapel, Sheepwash Lane, Great Bridge, Sunday School Anniversary, June 1915. Anniversaries in June have always been the highlight of the church year, and even more so in the early part of the last century, as this bulging platform shows. Among those on the back row are, fifth from left, Ernie York; second from right, Len Williams; front row, sixth from left: Rose Bissell; second from right: Doris Jones. (Rose Ward)

St Peter's church Festival in Great Bridge, 1 May 1921. This enormous procession can be seen winding its way from the canal bridge in Great Bridge Street to where they are just entering Slater Street. On the right of the picture, just visible, is the side entrance and foyer of the Palace Cinema. (Pat Redrup)

Another view of the St Peter's church Festival, 1 May 1921. This time the procession is shown moving along Whitehall Road past the Royal Oak pub, which is near the street lamp in the distance. On the left of the picture, just beyond the tree, is the Revd Frank Smith, Vicar of St Peter's. (St Peter's church)

Members of the St Luke's Mission church, New Road, Great Bridge, assemble in the Market Place during their anniversary celebrations of 1905. Built in 1901 to replace a temporary structure, the church was served until its closure in 1966 by the clergy and licensed lay staff of St Martin's in Lower Church Lane, Tipton. In the background of the picture the Limerick Inn has the landlord's name, Thomas Brennand, prominently displayed across the frontage. (Philip Evans)

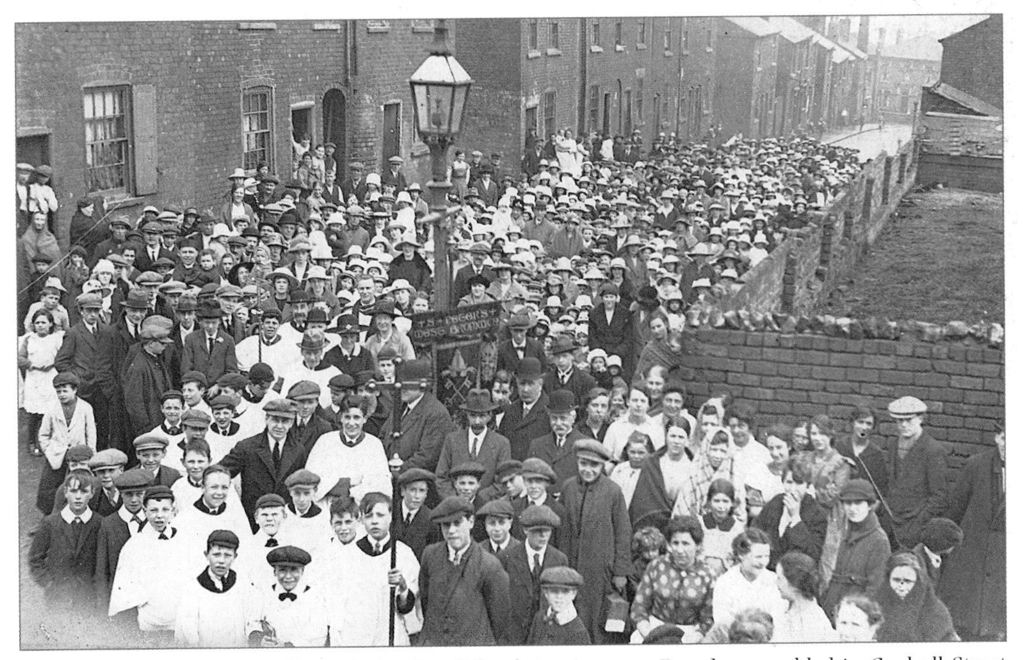

St Peter's church, Whitehall Road, Sunday School Anniversary Parade assembled in Cophall Street near the junction with Farley Street, *c.* 1920. This area has been known as 'Newtown' since the early nineteenth century when Farley and Horton Streets, together with a third one (since disappeared), were called Finch, Frances and Roger Streets. All of the properties seen here were demolished during the 1950s. (T.J.H. Price)

The pantomime cast of *Dick Whittington* pictured in the Sunday School room of Whitehall Road Primitive Methodist church, Greets Green, *c.* 1948. Back row, left to right: Ivy Round, Betty Tandy, Shirley Foster, Geoff Povey, Bill Downes, Brenda Arnold, Ron Downes, Jean Arnold, -?-, David Howes, Stan Dodd, Doreen Cox, Beattie Dodd, Colin Downes, Joyce Lester, Sid Wright, Ted Welch. Front row, standing: Hazel Jackson, Barry Hopson, Sheila Doughty, Douglas Cook, Celia Jones, Beryl Whitehouse, Anne Parkes, Iris Howes, Joan Smith, Sheila Tracey, Howard Baker, Jean Bushell. (Ivy Round-Hancock)

'The Evergreens' from Great Bridge Street Methodist church performing *Jack And The Beanstalk* at the Akrill Hall, West Bromwich, May 1966. In the centre of the picture on the back row is Ivy Round-Hancock, who has written and produced these pantomimes since 1933. The cast was Anne Round, Stan Dodd, Joan Howes, Michael Vaughan, Peter Best, Rona Cook, Joan Parsons, Ann Kirkpatrick, Margaret Smith, Diane Sheldon, Philip Tomlinson, Christine Harvey, Joyce Howes, Graham Simms, Jacqueline Morris, Geraldine Morgan, Marjorie Daw, Diane Williams, Jacqueline Bingham, Leslie Bingham, Jacqueline Harvey, Patricia Asbury, Jacqueline Best, Heather Sheldon, Gay Loftus and Diane Harvey. (Vera Morris)

The Great Bridge Street Primitive Methodists' production of the pantomime *Babes In The Wood*, *c*. 1960. Back row, left to right: -?-, -?-, John Fereday, Keith Stubbs, -?-, -?-, Elizabeth Addis, Brian Edmunds, Michael Burns, Barry Hopson. Middle row: Colin Downes, Michael Vaughan, Edwin Yates, Geoff Robinson, John Mander. Front row: -?-, Ivy Round, Barbara Tandy, -?-, Mary Howes, Jacqueline Joyce, Anne Round, Maureen Smith, Glynn Halford, Sheila Whitehouse, Linda Thompson, Diane Vaughan. (Ivy Round-Hancock)

On stage in the Sunday School room of Whitehall Road Primitive Methodist church, Greets Green, are the pantomime cast of *Little Red Riding Hood*, *c*. 1956. Front row, standing: -?-, Dorothy Mander, Diane Vaughan, Gillian Withers, Anne Round, Hazel Jackson, Joan Smith, Ivy Round, Colin Downes, Linda Thompson, Michael Vaughan. (Ivy Round-Hancock)

Barbara Breatt, Carnival Queen of St Peter's church, Whitehall Road, with attendant Olive Meek to her left, *c.* 1936. This was the first occasion that a vehicle was used to transport the queen and her entourage through the streets. In previous years they had to walk! Also pictured on the float are, front row, left to right: Sheila Walters, Gwen Martin, Joan Phillips, -?-, Doris Howell, Doris Burns. (Lily Phillips)

A superbly dressed group of concert party pierrots at the Salem Congregational church, Sheepwash Lane, Great Bridge, *c.* 1925. Back row, left to right: Jervoise Colclough, Leonard Williams, Lucy Jesson, Harry Jones, Beattie Williams, Eddie Ward, Cecil Brown. Front row: Gladys Holton, Cliff Ball, Arthur Brown, Edna Yates. Leonard Williams later became a missionary in Madagascar from 1934 to 1940 while Edna Yates' father was the owner of the Union Supply Co. in Great Bridge Market Place. (Annie Ball)

Jean Arnold, the 1945 Whitehall Road Primitive Methodist church Carnival Queen seen here with her attendants in Whitgreave Street, Greets Green. Left to right: Brenda Arnold, Jean Arnold, Doreen Cox, Dorothy Cooksey. The crowning ceremony took place, according to tradition, in the bandstand at Farley Park. (Jean Beddow)

A gathering of Carnival Queens past and present from Whitehall Road Primitive Methodist church, Greets Green, in Farley Park, 1947. Left to right: Brenda Arnold, 1947; Dorothy Cooksey, 1946; Jean Arnold, 1945; Marjorie Fieldhouse, 1941. (Ian Downes)

Toll End Early Morning School FC, 3 October 1948. Based at the local Toll End Adult School, they played their football in the Tipton League. Back row, left to right: T. Roberts, R. Hemmings, Bill Powell, Tom Harris, Sam Wood, Jim Durkin, Cyril Webb, B. Jenkins, Ken Knight. Front row: George Emms, Sid Griffiths, Les Barford, Cyril Jones, Jackie Hodgkins, Ernie Whitehouse, Alan Stokes. (Sid Griffiths)

The Mayor and Mayoress of West Bromwich, Councillor Joshua Churchman and his wife Violet, make a purchase from the fancy goods stall of the Salem Congregational church in Sheepwash Lane, October 1966. The Minister at the time was the Revd P.H. Goodwin, who reported that a record £250 was raised from the event, which was organised by Mr C.T. Ball. Back row, left to right: -?-, Rosalind Roberts, Janet Cartwright, Iris Rich, -?-, Elizabeth Bignell. (Joshua Churchman).

An outing from Great Bridge Street Primitive Methodist chapel to Trentham Gardens, *c.* 1950. Among those pictured are, front row: Michael Riley, Diane Burford, Trevor Jinks, Brian Edmunds; second row: Cynthia Clark, Doreen Riley, Michael Kennett; third row: Jean Riley, Ann Jones, Audrey Maull, Raymond Jinks, Patrick Williams; fourth row: William Riley, Ann Riley, Janet Downing; fifth row: Mrs Maull, Mrs Williams. (Doreen Boucher)

Elwell Street, Great Bridge, before joining the St Peter's church Carnival Parade, *c.* 1927. This group contains no fewer than seven members of the Markham family. Dorothy Markham is in the top hat; Daisy Markham is third from left in the middle row. Front row, left to right: Ernie Markham, N. Markham, -?-, Gwen Markham, -?-, -?-, Len Markham, Joseph G. Markham. (Ron Markham)

St Peter's church, Whitehall Road, Great Bridge, *c.* 1925. Built at a cost of £4,000 in 1857, it was finally completed and consecrated on 29 June 1858 by the Bishop of Lichfield, the Rt Revd John Lonsdale. Three years later, in 1861, the parish boundaries were redrawn to include Greets Green and Great Bridge, the first Vicar being the Revd Charles Massey, who had succeeded the Priest in Charge, the Revd James Bradshaw. In November 1966 the church came close to being totally destroyed when it was severely damaged by fire. (Philip Evans)

The Revd Frank A. Smith, Vicar of St Peter's church, Whitehall Road, Great Bridge, from 1916 until 1925. An immensely popular vicar, he was an ardent socialist with a strong social conscience and had a deep concern for the unemployed and poor of the parish. Apparently he used to give away the proceeds from concerts to families in need before the money could be spent on new hymn books, kneelers or whatever else was needed in the church school. It was during his incumbency that the Church Army Social Centre was opened. In 1925 he left to become Vicar of St Michael's at Brierley Hill, where he spent six years before his eventual death in October 1931. Such was the great affection for him that hundreds of townspeople attended his funeral and the church, which had a seating capacity of 1,200 was filled to overflowing. His interment took place at Hartshill Cemetery, Stoke-on-Trent. (Joan Devaney)

The Revd Lancelot John Lamplugh, Vicar of St Peter's church, Whitehall Road, Great Bridge, from 1925 until 1961. Ordained in 1908, he was a descendant of Thomas Lamplugh, who was Archbishop of York at the end of the seventeenth century. Both Lancelot's father and uncle were also priests. A bachelor, he was Curate of Christ Church, Coseley in 1914, later becoming Vicar before moving on to serve in Wednesbury. In 1925 he began the longest of St Peter's incumbencies lasting thirty-six years, during which period the Sunday School, Guild and Tennis Club flourished. He was an academic man, and when he died in April 1961 at the age of seventy-eight, a memorial window was placed in the sanctuary depicting St Anselm the Theologian. He was at home in Great Bridge, and so it was no surprise when he left instructions for his burial to be in St Peter's churchyard. (St Peter's church)

A rear view of St Peter's church vicarage, Whitehall Road, Great Bridge, *c.* 1902. Until this house was built in 1898 by the Revd Henry Jesson, mostly at his own expense, the Vicars had for the previous forty years lived at a variety of addresses as far afield as Old Meeting Street, Great Bridge Street, Sheepwash Lane and Fisher Street. (T.J.H. Price)

The frontage of what remained of the New Road Methodist church, Great Bridge, after it was completely destroyed by enemy bombing on 17 May 1941. Pictured here in 1956, the poster proclaiming 'At last we re-build' is a reference to a new church hall which was shortly to be built in nearby Mount Street. The hall was opened on Saturday 21 September 1957 by the Revd J. Courtenay Jacobs accompanied by the Mayor of Tipton, Alderman W.H. Hirons JP. It was also dedicated for worship by the Revd W. Russell Shearer MA. (Jean Carter)

The Methodist New Connexion church, New Road, Great Bridge, *c.* 1905. As a result of internal troubles in the Wesleyan Methodist Church, in 1797 Alexander Kilham formed a new church community which subsequently became known as New Connexionists and later United Methodists. The first church of this community was erected at Dudley Port in 1836 and had a day and Sunday school attached. Others followed until on 14 March 1864 a memorial foundation stone was laid for the New Connexion chapel in New Road, Great Bridge. Built at a cost of £1,400 and seating 800 people, the chapel opened on 12 May 1865. In 1867 the resident minister was recorded as being the Revd J. Pyle. On 17 May 1941 during a German bombing raid over Tipton the church was completely destroyed, and it was not until 1971 that a replacement was built on the site. (Ken Rock)

Salem chapel, Sheepwash Lane, Great Bridge, *c.* 1925. Built in 1839 at a cost of £800, the chapel was of stuccoed brick in a classical style. Previously worship had taken place at a variety of locations, until in 1833 meetings were being held in a room in Blades Street, which ran between Brickhouse Lane and Great Bridge Street, where the Asda supermarket now stands. On 1 January 1834 a small preaching house was opened in Sheepwash Lane built at a cost of £262, including £57 for the land. Exactly a year later the Congregational Church Fellowship was formally constituted, and as numbers increased services were held in the new infants' school which had just been erected at a cost of £165. The first resident minister in 1838 was the Revd Mr Newton, who was succeeded by the Revd D. Morgan around 1840. On 11 June 1932, a hundred years after the formation of the church, a new assembly hall was opened by Mrs Arthur C. Harrison. The chapel closed in 1972 and was demolished two years later. (Ken Rock)

Aston Street Primitive Methodist chapel at its junction with Toll End Road, 2 August 1968. Built in 1847 to serve the expanding community of Toll End, the chapel was active for a period of 120 years, until in 1967 it closed owing to declining membership. The church was demolished in 1970. (Alan Price)

The demolition of Wesley Methodist chapel, Great Bridge. Built in 1840 to replace an earlier structure, which itself had been on the site since 1811, the chapel was apparently served by two ministers. They were the Revd James E. Moulton and the Resident Minister Nehemiah Cumock, to whom a son was born in March of that year. It was this son who later became the editor of the *Methodist Recorder*. In April 1970, after a hundred and thirty years of worship, the chapel was finally pulled down and later replaced by a bank. (Alan Price)

Whitehall Road Primitive Methodist chapel, Greets Green, *c*. 1955. Built in 1848 to seat 360 people at a cost of £1400, this chapel was originally part of the Darlaston Circuit, which included the whole of the Black Country. In 1849 the chapel became part of the newly formed West Bromwich Circuit, which at that time included Tipton. At the back of the chapel were schoolrooms, which between 1872 and 1932 were frequently hired by the nearby Board School because of overcrowding. When cracks started to appear in the walls the chapel became unsafe, and it was demolished around 1957. (Michael Vaughan)

The 7th Tipton Cubs pictured in the playground of their group headquarters at Fisher Street Schools, *c.* 1955. Scouting was introduced to the Great Bridge area in October 1928 by corn and seed merchant Bernard Duckworth, with boys being accepted from the age of eight as Cubs and from eleven into the Scouts. At the back of the group are Cub Mistresses Brenda Marsh and Rita Richards (hidden). Among those in the back row are Roderick Hill, Barry Stokes and Ken Cox; in the front row, second and third from the left, are Cliff Price and Jeff Roper. (Cliff Price)

Children and staff at Greets Green Infants School during the presentation of a certificate commemorating their fifty years in the National Savings movement, November 1966. The certificate is being received from the Mayor of West Bromwich, Councillor Joshua Churchman JP, by Anita Snape and Ian Fisher. The school, under headmistress Miss M. Whitton, had only 150 pupils at the time but they still managed to buy around £12-worth of savings stamps each week. (Joshua Churchman)

St Peter's Council School, Greets Green as it appeared at the time it was transferred to the Local Authority, 1910. Previously a national school dating from 1866, this Venetian Gothic-style two-storey building stood in Whitehall Road between St Peter's church and Farley Park. It replaced an earlier school which in 1859 had been housed in a small corrugated-iron building adjoining the church. At its peak the school had an average attendance of around 400 pupils but by the time of its closure in 1932, when the new George Salter School opened, the numbers had fallen well below that figure. The school building was demolished in 1964 and by 1966 the new St Peter's church hall had been opened on the site. (T.J.H. Price)

Fisher Street School, pictured here around 1905, was built on the West Bromwich side of Great Bridge in 1859. Curiously, however, it was intended to serve the nearby Wesleyan Methodist chapel which was itself situated in the Tipton parish. The first Headmaster was Joseph Pollard but in 1865 he was succeeded by Joseph Vincent, whose wife Margaret became Headmistress of the Infants Department. Following the transfer to Local Authority control in 1907 the senior pupils were, in 1932, moved to the new George Salter School in West Bromwich. Fisher Street Infants and Junior School finally closed in 1969. (Keith Hodgkins)

A view of Greets Green Board School, Whitehall Road, showing the separate entrances for boys and girls, *c.* 1905. The school opened in 1876 and by 1890 new classrooms were being added to meet the demand for places. This was still not enough and a room at the nearby Primitive Methodist chapel had to be hired to provide even more accommodation, a situation which lasted until 1932. With pupil numbers declining, the boys' and girls' departments were merged in 1938 to form a mixed junior and infants school. The school closed in 1969 and was demolished in December 1972. (Joyce Stimpson)

Golds Hill Board School from the junior playground, *c.* 1911. Built in 1855 by Messrs Bagnall & Sons, it was mainly intended for their employees' children although others were allowed to attend. Because of financial difficulties the Bagnalls sold the building to the West Bromwich School Board who, after enlarging and carrying out improvements, re-opened it in 1878. The school became a junior mixed and infants school in 1911, which continued until 1949 when the infants were moved to Harvilles Hawthorn. The school closed in 1950 after the junior pupils were also transferred there. (Iris Reynolds)

Teaching staff at Fisher Street School, Great Bridge, *c.* 1950. Headmistress Lucy Swinnerton, seated centre, had succeeded Lilian Sanders in 1938, having previously been in charge at Holy Trinity Infants School, West Bromwich. In 1954 she moved to Charlemont School, also in West Bromwich, from where she eventually retired in 1964. Back row, left to right: Grace Watkins, Betty Davies, Lily Weaver, Tony Baker, Mary Hartshorne. Front row: Anita Ford, Vera Bamford, Lucy Swinnerton, Frank Wooton, Bertha Griffiths. (Lily Weaver)

Headmistress Monica Richards, seated centre, and the teaching staff of Fisher Street School, *c.* 1964. Miss Richards, who succeeded Lucy Swinnerton in 1954, was to remain at Fisher Street until its closure in 1969 and in doing so became only the fifth headmistress to hold the position in the school's 110-year history. Back row, left to right: Len Edwards, Dolly Holland, Bertha Griffiths, Norman Riley. Front row: Rita Hallard, Doreen Eden, Monica Richards, Diane Wadsworth, Molly Boughton. (Monica Richards)

A rare photograph of the teaching staff at St Peter's Council School, Whitehall Road, Great Bridge, *c.* 1928. Those pictured outside the school building, which closed in 1932, include on the back row, left to right: -?-, Miss Squires, Miss Alys Standing. Front row: -?-, Miss Southern (Headmistress), -?-, Miss Wilkinson. (Moreen Wilkes)

The teaching staff of Great Bridge School, Mount Street, *c.* 1972. Seated in the centre of the picture is Headmistress Monica Richards, who occupied the position from 1969 until 1974. She served a further six years at the Joseph Turner School before retiring in 1980. Back row, left to right: Ann Waring, Jenny ?, Christine Biot, Peggy Patrick, Pat ?, Paul Bailey. Front row: Jackie Smart, Lily Roberts, Monica Richards, Ken Bates, -?-. (Monica Richards)

A very young Lilian Sanders is pictured here in 1898 at the start of her teaching career in the 'mixed' department of Fisher Street School. When the Headmistress of the infants' department, Margaret Vincent, retired in 1906 she was succeeded in the post by Miss Sanders. In 1930 Lilian was appointed Headmistress of both the infants and the 'mixed' departments following the retirement of Mr R.J. Powis, who had himself succeeded Joseph Vincent in 1909. She retired from teaching in 1938, her successor being Lucy Ellen Swinnerton. (Peter Coley)

Miss Yates' class at Fisher Street School, Great Bridge, *c.* 1928. Back row, left to right: -?-, Philip Branson, Bill Reid, Oliver Holton, Eric Gardner, Les Bailey. Fifth row: Fred Venables, Bertie Glover, Jim Molloy, Marjory Aston, -?-, Billy Mann, Sam Bowen, Leslie Charlton, -?-. Fourth row: Evelyn Smith, Joyce Williams, Kathy Burton, Sarah Sheldon, Leslie Nichols, Alf Burns, Leslie ?, -?-. Third row: Olive Fletcher, Ruth Morris, Vera Morris, -?-, Claude ?, Sam Reid, Winnie Rolfe, -?-. Second row: Ronnie Walford, Dorothy Corbett, Evelyn Robinson, Edna Downs, Gladys Whitehouse, Dorothy Ore, Muriel Foster, Bertha George, -?-. Front row: John Turner, Lucy Cook, Hilda Brookes, Hilda Gopsil, Jimmy Hemmings, Rhoda Basford, Evelyn Wright, -?-, -?-. (Vera Morris)

Miss Lilian Sanders, Headmistress, and Miss Peplow from Fisher Street School, Great Bridge, pose for a photograph with their pupils during a day out to the Abberley Valley in Worcestershire, 1932. Back row, left to right: George Gopsil, -?-, -?-, ? Smith, Lilian Sanders, Ray Markham, -?-, -?-, -?-, Miss Peplow, ? Downes. Middle row: Nellie Aston, Mary Bedowes, Jean Bell, Pearl Holmes, Ruby Holmes, Sybil Price, Doreen Horton. Front row: Florrie Turner, Roseley Wilkes, Alice Ball, Joyce Howes, Irene ?, Olive Daulman. Lying on the grass: Arthur Griffiths, -?-. (Sybil Price)

Pupils in Mrs Lily Weaver's top class at Fisher Street School, Great Bridge, making festive hats in preparation for the Christmas party of 1953. In the centre background can be seen the open door of Headmistress Lucy Swinnerton's office. Two years later, in 1955, Mrs Weaver moved to Charlemont School, thus ending a seventeen-year association with Fisher Street going back to 1938. (Lily Weaver)

Children in a mixed infants class at Great Bridge School, Mount Street, *c.* 1948. Among the pupils pictured are, left of centre in the striped jersey, Alan Ball, and second from top right, Terry Hyde. The pupils received their tuition from Mrs Wylde, the headmaster at the time being William Nock. (Annie Ball)

Christmas decorations adorn a classroom at Great Bridge School, Mount Street, in December 1953. The party hats had no doubt been made by the pupils themselves, who include Linda Smith, Pat Guest, Geraldine Lloyd, Valerie Edwards, Linda Cashmore, Mary Hans and Eunice Smith. (Val Harris)

The children of Class 1 with their books open at Greets Green Board School, *c.* 1931. Pupil George Morris is on the extreme right of the fourth row from the front. Until 1932, when George Salter School opened, senior boys and girls from Fisher Street and St Peter's Schools were transferred here for secondary education. (Vera Morris)

Pupils of St Peter's School, Whitehall Road, Great Bridge, photographed after performing a play on the vicarage lawn, *c.* 1931. Back row, left to right: -?-, Florence Davis, -?-, Audrey Turner, Gladys Baker, Joe Ashcroft, Mary Stockel, Jim Cowley, Joan Morris, ? Woodward. Second row: Jim Dugmore, -?-, ? Stockley, -?-, Ernie Broad, Phoebe Westwood, Bill Nicholson, -?-, -?-, -?-, Madge Heath. Third row: Jonah Bratt, -?-, Mary Calloway, -?-, -?-, Eva Reeves, -?-, -?-, Joshua Churchman, -?-, -?-, Douglas Dugmore, ? Howell. Front row: ? Monk, Billy Payne, fourth from right: Jack Heath. (Muriel Ashcroft)

A very early Fisher Street School infants class performing their interpretation of *Little Miss Muffet*, *c.* 1914. The title role was played by Elsie Pritchard, who is second from the left in the middle row. To her right is Cyril Hodson, while on her left is Gladys Holloway, Nellie Reynolds and Marjorie Cashmore. Front row, left to right: Gertie Meek, Cyril Smith, -?-, Jackie Aston, -?-. The teacher at the time was a Miss Powell. (Elsie Pritchard)

Girls at Fisher Street School, Great Bridge, practise country dancing in their specially made outfits, *c.* 1933. Third from the left of the picture is Clara Cartwright, fourth from the left is Violet Hickinbotham, and fifth from the left is Pauline Price. Behind the wall in the background is the bowling green of the Stork Inn. (Pauline Parfitt)

Children taking part in pageants were very much part of the social calendar in local schools, and Fisher Street in Great Bridge was no exception: this picture dates from about 1934. Back row, left to right: -?-, Pauline Price, -?-, Melvyn Douglas, Brenda Hill, John King, Jean Sowery, Violet Clark. Front row: Ron George, Sam Price, Jack Wright. (Sam Price)

Pictured in the playground of Fisher Street School, Great Bridge, are pupils from the cast of a play based on the legend of Androcles and the Lion, *c.* 1930. Back row, left to right: Ray Addis, Les Bailey, -?-, Fred Venables, Lawrence Wright, Oliver Holton, -?-, Ronnie Walford, -?-. Front row: Eric Harper, Teddy Bunch, Philip Branson, -?-, Sammy Green. (Elizabeth Bignell)

A concert at the Fisher Street Schools, Great Bridge, *c.* 1960. These were usually held in the large assembly area which formed two separate classrooms when the dividing partition was closed. Back row, left to right: Susan Sutton, Christine Ellis, Jane Hughes, Diane Tedstone, June Merchant. Middle row: Gillian Waters, Carol Hughes, Jacqueline Bingham. Front row: Catherine Dixon, -?-, Pamela Roberts, Glynis Lloyd, Christine Davies. (Janet Hughes)

The girls' netball team of Fisher Street School, Great Bridge, in the playground with their teacher Chris Lloyd after the 1965/6 season. Back row, left to right: Chris Lloyd, Glenys Mills, Diane Bagley, Janice Johnson. Front row: Jill Hughes, Sandra Corbett, Diane Homer, Susan Whitehouse, Diane Jackson. (Janet Hughes)

The Fisher Street School, Great Bridge, football team, 1960/1. Deputy Headmaster Frank Wooton is the man credited with starting these football teams at the school during the mid-1950s. He joined Fisher Street just after serving in the RAF during the Second World War, in which he was awarded the DFC. Back row, left to right: Michael Green, Michael Darby, Billy Walls, Frank Wooton, David Hamblett, Melvyn Abraham, Graham Whale. Front row: Alan Dunn, Raymond Hickman, Gary Parkes, Trevor Hickinbotham, John Hunt. (Monica Richards)

School football teams had not been going long at Fisher Street, Great Bridge, when this photograph was taken, *c.* 1956. Their home ground was Ratcliffs in Dial Lane, Hill Top, West Bromwich. Back row, left to right: Jimmy Gittins, Trevor Allen, George Harris, John Green, Arthur Cook, Keith Woodbine. Front row: David Fullard, Barry Nicholls, John Lyman, Roderick Hill, Cliff Price, Michael Farley, Jeff Roper. (Cliff Price)

Members of Greets Green Junior School football team, *c.* 1929. The school produced many outstanding soccer players who achieved professional status, such as Reg and 'Toddy' Bowen, Ken Hodgkisson and brothers Bill and Sammy Richardson. Pictured on the back row, extreme right, is Cecil Palmer, with Jacky Burns next to him. (Hilda Palmer)

Greets Green Junior School Headmaster Mr T.G. Summerton, standing centre, with the school football team, 1952. The team played against other schools in the West Bromwich area on a league basis, their home ground being Greets Green Rec. Team: back row, left to right: Keith Sinar, Brian Ford, Dennis Roden, Ray Law, Archie Penn, Eddie Jones, Roy Taylor. Front row: Victor Markham, Keith Markham, Gordon Weston, Horace Burgess, ? Wilson. (Gordon Weston)

CHAPTER SIX

TRANSPORT

A Birmingham Corporation tramcar waits outside Lloyds Bank, Great Bridge, 9 August 1938. What appears to be a No. 76 on short working from Birmingham to Great Bridge is, in fact, a normal route 74 car with passengers waiting to continue their journey towards Dudley. The photographer, W.A. Camwell, who enjoyed taking pictures of trams displaying unusual destinations, had persuaded the driver to alter the number. In 1884 a regular steam tram service from Birmingham to Great Bridge commenced, replacing the unreliable horse-drawn service which had ceased in 1876 after operating for only four years. (National Tramway Museum)

Great Bridge South passenger railway station, showing a train arriving from the direction of Swan Village, 17 June 1963. Opened in 1866, the station, which was on the GWR Birmingham to Dudley line, had its passenger service suspended from 1915 to 1920 in order to release staff and plant for essential war purposes. In June 1964 the station finally closed to passengers, with goods traffic ceasing by 1968. (Ned Williams)

Great Bridge North railway station, showing the parcel and booking offices left and centre, with the waiting rooms to the right of the picture, *c.* 1961. Although the station dealt mainly with goods traffic, a passenger service did operate on this line between Dudley and Walsall. The station, which was on the South Staffordshire line, opened in 1850 and was gradually phased out during the 1960s. (Nigel Hazelwood)

A passenger train hauled by a 5100 class 2–6–2T heads towards Great Bridge station on the GWR line from Swan Village, 18 May 1963. Just beyond the carriages in the distance can be seen the Top Beehive pub, while on the right of the picture is Brickhouse Lane. The track was also bordered on the left by an area known locally as 'The Cracker' which in 1865 was the location of Frederick Deeley's Roman Cement works. (David Wilson)

Signalman Fred Shirley looks out from the Great Bridge North signal box on the South Staffordshire line, with the New Road bridge in the background, *c.* 1961. The track to the right continues under the bridge to the Horseley Fields junction. The signal box was a standard LNWR design and was operated by three men, each working an eight-hour shift system, six days a week. (Nigel Hazelwood)

A Birmingham Corporation No. 74 bus on the Birmingham–Dudley route leaving Great Bridge Market Place, 24 February 1963. Next to Dewhurst the butcher's, grocer George Briscoe occupies the shop known previously as the Home and Colonial Tea Stores. The distant building on the left of the picture with the curved roof was, in the 1930s, a motor repair business run by A. Hadlington & Sons Ltd, who also owned the Dartmouth Garage, West Bromwich. (David Wilson)

An ex-West Bromwich Daimler bus in the new livery of West Midlands Passenger Transport Executive waits on the bridge over the Haines Branch canal in Great Bridge, 31 May 1975. The old canalside cottages to the right of the picture were built at about the same time as the opening of this canal in 1833. (David Wilson)

An unusual view of a Birmingham Corporation No. 74 bus on the Birmingham–Dudley service passing Kingfisher Ltd at the top of Charles Street, Great Bridge, *c.* 1962. Because of roadworks to 'Roberts's Bridge' in Great Bridge Street, the Dudley-bound service had been diverted at Swan Village via Phoenix Street. Buses travelling from Dudley to Birmingham, however, continued to use the Great Bridge Street route. (David Wilson)

Great Bridge Street at the junction of Richmond Street, March 1963. The No. 74 service was jointly operated by the Birmingham and West Bromwich Corporation, under an agreement which brought to an end the tramway era in West Bromwich on 1 April 1939. (David Wilson)

The eight locks on the Walsall canal looking towards Great Bridge from Ryders Green Road, 7 January 1967. The narrowboat laden with coal is being operated by 'Caggy' Stevens, pictured here with his horse Mac. The small opening to the right of the boat leads to a wharf which served the firm of Kingfisher Ltd in Charles Street. (David Wilson)

Accidents involving narrow boats and horses were an occupational hazard in the canal era, as this picture taken in December 1966 shows. The horse is being rescued from the Great Bridge Street section of the Walsall canal looking towards Ryders Green. Firemen from the West Bromwich Brigade are seen here directing operations, which necessitated the draining of this part of the canal. (David Wilson)

The Great Bridge sawmills of Thomas Cox & Sons Ltd, timber and slate merchants who were situated just off the Market Place alongside the Haines Branch Canal, *c.* 1910. The firm, which was established in 1828, also described itself as Belfast Roofing contractors as well as suppliers of timber to wheelwrights and coffin makers. Imported timber was transported on barges via the River Thames to Brentford, where narrowboats of the type pictured here would complete the journey to the Midlands. In the late 1950s the company became Tailby & Cox Ltd and by 1970 had ceased trading altogether. (T.J.H. Price)

For over thirty years this 1930 Morris Commercial lorry was used by Billy Hyde to transport fresh fruit and vegetables from the Birmingham Wholesale Market to his fruiterer's shop at 248 Great Bridge Street. The business was established in 1868 by Billy's grandmother, Mary Sheldon, who in about 1916 bequeathed it to her son-in-law Richard Hyde. In 1926 the next door property at No. 250, also owned by the Hyde family, was converted into a tobacconist's which operated alongside the fruiterer's until they both closed in 1963. (Ernest Hyde)

Albert Hodson, dairyman, in Slater Street, Great Bridge, on his 550cc New Hudson Model 2 motor-cycle with a Watsonian milk float sidecar attachment, *c.* 1933. This milk delivery round, which covered the Great Bridge and Greets Green areas, was the forerunner of his corn and seed merchant's business opened in 1937 at 6 New Road. (Philip Evans)

A familiar sight on the roads of Toll End in 1920 was John Price of Bridge Road with his motor-cycle and sidecar, pictured here with Cotterills fields in the background. The machine was a Redditch-made 1913 Royal Enfield motor-cycle combination, model 180. The 770cc V-twin engine was, in fact, made by the London firm of J.A. Prestwich and had only two gears. The combination, which had a petrol tank capacity of just 2 gallons, cost 80 guineas when purchased new. (T.J.H. Price)

A West Bromwich Corporation bus, seen here in Whitehall Road operating on the Great Bridge to Oldbury route via Greets Green, *c.* 1926. The service was introduced in October 1925 and extended to Hill Top one month later. The 40hp Tilling-Stevens TS3 bus, which had a petrol-electric transmission, was also one of the first vehicles to display the new blue and cream livery. (Ken Rock)

Steam locomotives waiting to be dismantled at the firm of John Cashmore Ltd, Bagnall Street, Golds Hill, June 1961. Known as 'Honest John' Cashmore because of his fair dealing, he established his scrap metal business in Mill Street, Horseley Heath, in 1872. By 1911 he had opened a second branch at Newport, Monmouthshire, where obsolete warships were being broken up for scrap. Two years later in 1913 came the move to Golds Hill, where extensive premises were erected opposite Golds Hill Schools. On 5 May 1932, after only three years in retirement, he died at his home in Ballfields, Great Bridge aged ninety-two. (Derek Allen)

ACKNOWLEDGEMENTS

I would like to express my thanks to everyone who loaned me photographs, without whose support this publication would not have been possible. Every contributor has been individually acknowledged at the end of each caption. My gratitude is also extended to the people listed below who provided me with additional information and assistance during the production of this book.

Doris Abbotts, David Allway, Elizabeth Bignell, Ian Bott, Jess Bowen, John Brimble, Jean Carter, Fran Cartwright, Keith Cherrington, Joshua Churchman, Arthur Cole, Peter Coley, David Cormell, Pat Davy, Janice Endean, Philip Evans, Stan Hill, Keith Hodgkins, Ken Hodgkisson, Janet Hughes, Walter Kendall, Mary Law, David Marshall, Tony Matthews, Geoffrey May, Vera Morris, Albert Murphy, Geoffrey Paddock, Chris Patterson, Robin Pearson, Alan Price, Clifford Price, Geoffrey Price, Jack Randle, Monica Richards, Ken Rock, Ivy Round-Hancock, Dorothy Smith, Brian Walker, Ned Williams, Peter Willis, David Wilson, Glyn Wilton, George Woodbine.

I am also grateful to: *Birmingham Post & Mail*, Black Country Living Museum, Black Country Society, Dudley Libraries, Eardley Lewis, Hughes & Holmes Ltd, National Tramway Museum, Sandwell Libraries, Sandwell Community History & Archive Centre, South Staffs Water Co., Tipton Camera Club, Tipton Civic Society, Vintage Motor Cycle Club Ltd, Walsall Local History Centre, *Wolverhampton Express & Star*. My special thanks to Kathleen Homeshaw for typing the manuscript. Many of the photographs used in this book were processed by Edwin Yates who freely gave of his time and expertise, and to whom I am most grateful. Thanks also to Dr Carl Chinn, whose support is much appreciated.

Finally, to my wife Beryl for her encouragement and patience.

THE BLACK COUNTRY SOCIETY

This voluntary society, affiliated to the Civic Trust, was founded in 1967 as a reaction to the trend of the late 1950s and early 1960s to amalgamate everything into large units and in the Midlands to sweep away the area's industrial heritage in the process.

The general aim of the Society is to create interest in the past, present and future of the Black Country, and early on it campaigned for the establishment of an industrial museum. In 1975 the Black Country Living Museum was started by Dudley Borough Council on 26 acres of totally derelict land adjoining the grounds of Dudley Castle. This has developed into an award-winning museum which attracts over 250,000 visitors annually.

It was announced in August 1998 that having secured a lottery grant of nearly £3 million, the Museum Board will be able to authorize the start of work on a £4.5 million state-of-the-art interpretation centre. This will be known as the 'Rolfe Street Project', named after the street which once housed the Smethwick Baths. The façade of this Victorian building is to be incorporated into the new interpretation centre.

At the Black Country Living Museum there is a boat dock fully equipped to restore narrowboats of wood and iron and different vessels can be seen on the dock throughout the year. From behind the Bottle and Glass Inn visitors can travel on a canal boat into Dudley Canal Tunnel, a memorable journey to see spectacular limestone caverns and the fascinating Castle Mill Basin.

There are 2,500 members of the Black Country Society and all receive the quarterly magazine *The Blackcountryman*, of which 124 issues have been published since its founding in 1967. In the whole collection there are some 1,800 authoritative articles on all aspects of the Black Country by historians, teachers, researchers, students, subject experts and ordinary folk with an extraordinary story to tell. The whole constitutes a unique resource about the area and is a mine of information for students and researchers who frequently refer to it. Many schools and libraries are subscribers. Three thousand copies of the magazine are printed each quarter. It is non-commercial, and contributors do not receive payment for their articles.

PO Box 71 · Kingswinford · West Midlands DY6 9YN